SINGING BETWEEN THE LINES

FIFTEEN-MINUTE MUSIC THEORY LESSONS FOR YOUR CHURCH CHOIR

GINGER G. WYRICK

Abingdon Press
Nashville

Singing Between the Lines
Fifteen-Minute Music Theory Lessons for Your Church Choir

Copyright © 2006 Abingdon Press

This book is printed on acid-free, recycled paper.

ISBN 0-687-49748-5

06 07 08 09 10 11 12 13 14 15— 10 9 8 7 6 5 4 3 2 1

MANUFACTURED IN THE UNITED STATES OF AMERICA

CONTENTS

HYMN TUNES

ADORO TE DEVOTE	Plainsong
AMEN, AMEN	African American spiritual
ANTIOCH	Arranged from G. F. Handel, 1741, by Lowell Mason, 1848
BEALOTH	From Mason's *Sacred Harp,* 1843
BEECHER	John Zundel, 1870
BRADBURY	William B. Bradbury, 1859
DARWALL'S 148TH	John Darwall, 1770; harm. from *Hymns Ancient and Modern,* 1875, alt.
DEO GRACIAS	English melody; harm. from *Hymns Ancient and Modern,* Revised, 1950
DUKE STREET	John Hatton, 1793
EASTER HYMN	*Lyra Davidica,* 1708
EBENEZER	Thomas J. Williams, 1890
GLORIA	French carol
GREENSLEEVES	16th century English melody
HAMBURG	Lowell Mason, 1824
HERZLIEBSTER JESU	Johann Crüger, 1640
HURSLEY	*Katholisches Gesangbuch,* ca. 1774; adapted from *Metrical Psalter,* 1855
HYMN TO JOY	Ludwig van Beethoven, 1824; arranged by Edward Hodges, 1864
I AM THINE	William H. Doane, 1875
IN DIR IST FREUDE	Giovanni Giacomo Gastoldi, 1593
IN DULCI JUBILO	German melody
IRBY	Henry J. Gauntlett, 1849
JESU, JOY OF MAN'S DESIRING	Johann Schop, arranged by J. S. Bach, 1723
JESUS LOVES ME	William B. Bradbury, 1862
LAUDA ANIMA	John Goss, 1869
LEAD ME, LORD	Samuel Sebastian Wesley, 1861
MARTYRDOM	Attributed to Hugh Wilson, 1827
MARYTON	H. Percy Smith, 1874
MORECAMBE	Frederick C. Atkinson, 1870
NETTLETON	Wyeth's *Repository of Sacred Music, Part Second,* 1813
REST	Frederick C. Maker, 1887
ST. AGNES	John B. Dukes, 1866
ST. CHRYSOSTOM	Joseph Barnby
ST. THEODULPH	Melchior Teschner, 1615; harm. by W. H. Monk, 1861
STEAL AWAY	African American spiritual
STUTTGART	Attributed to C. F. Witt, 1715; adapted by Henry J. Gauntlett, 1861
THOMPSON	Will L. Thompson, 1880
TRENTHAM	Robert Jackson, 1888
UNSER HERRSCHER	Joachim Neander, 1680
WINCHESTER OLD	From Este's *Whole Booke of Psalmes,* 1592
WORDS OF LIFE	Philip P. Bliss, 1874

INTRODUCTION

Welcome to the world of teaching your choir to read music. This beautiful universal language spans cultures, languages, and time—allowing the world to communicate through sound. The fundamentals of music theory are unchanging, making this a great tool for improving your choir's skill level. What they will learn applies to all types of music making, including choral and instrumental. Music will come alive for your choir once they understand what they are seeing on the page. Rehearsals are productive, ensemble members are more confident, and the final product is better.

Hymns are used throughout the book to illustrate the musical concepts. The hymn appears in the session worksheet as part of the application process. The hymn tune and suggested hymn texts are included in each session.

Feel free to modify each lesson to your own teaching style. Use illustrations from your experience to introduce concepts. Include your choir members in the teaching process. Many of your participants may have had some music background, such as piano lessons, and will enjoy contributing to the process. Most of all, have fun!

ORGANIZATION

The Book:
- Thirty lessons are included.
- Each lesson is about 15 minutes.
- Lessons are presented in order, building on previous concepts.

The Worksheets:
- Provide the Music Application segment.
- There is one worksheet provided per lesson.
- May be completed as part of the class or sent home.

Materials Needed:
- Piano
- Board (white board/dry erase markers; chalkboard/chalk; or flip chart/markers)
- Paper and pencil for participants
- Step bells (optional)
- Metronome (optional)

How to Use the Book with Your Choir

As a part of a choir rehearsal:
1. Teach one lesson per week in rehearsal (15 minutes).
2. Meet 15 minutes before rehearsal with those wishing to participate.

As a separate class:
1. Meet 30 minutes each week.
   - Teach one session.
   - Do worksheet together.
   - Omit "In Rehearsal" and use with the entire choir.

2. Meet 30 minutes each week.
   - Teach two sessions.
   - Send worksheets home.
   - Omit "In Rehearsal" and use with the entire choir.

3. Meet 45 minutes to 1 hour each week.
   - Teach two sessions.
   - Do worksheets together.
   - Omit "In Rehearsal" and use with the entire choir.

Concept: Teaching focus for the lesson

This is the lesson in a nutshell. Think of how you could explain and demonstrate each concept in your own words. If you are unsure of any concept in that lesson, refer to the Concept Corner at the end of the lesson, a music dictionary, online sources, or another musical colleague for additional information.

Preparation

A list of things to do before class identifies which worksheet is used in that session and reminds you to make copies for your participants. Some lessons include an activities chart you may write on the board prior to class in order to save time.

Materials

It is suggested that you use a metronome and step bells. These items are optional. Feel free to include your own resources to supplement the lesson. Consult a local music store or an online resource to compare style and price. Step bells are available for purchase through a local music supply store or many online resources. This tool sets small chime bars on a staircase form to demonstrate melodic movement. It effectively shows the distance relationship of pitches.

Teaching Method

A suggested outline is offered to present the material. The ideas provide a method to order your presentation. Add your own words and ideas to make each session unique. Suggestions may include illustrations, definitions, and demonstrations. You can then determine how you will teach the material.

Music Application: Worksheet

A worksheet is provided based on the concepts in the session. Review the worksheet prior to the session so that you may explain each element and answer questions. Each worksheet includes a review of the concepts, whether to write, identify, or define them, with some form of application. Hymns are used throughout this curriculum to introduce both musical ideas and hymn tunes. The hymn tune is identified in the Music Application section and includes common texts associated with it. Consider incorporating the hymn tune into your rehearsal to build your choir's repertoire. Answer Keys are provided for you to check the participant's progress (see page 82). You may post the answer key so that each person can check their work privately or collect the sheets and check them yourself. If you do the sheets in class, follow up with a group answer time.

Ear Training (pages 68-78)

Provides an activity to enhance hearing, recognizing, and applying the musical concepts. This may be simple aural identification, aural memory, or writing exercises. Examples may need to be written on the board or they may be included at the bottom of the worksheet. Review each activity and practice demonstrating before the session. You may incorporate your own activities or modify these to build aural skills.

In Rehearsal

Suggestions are provided here on how to apply the concepts in your choir practice. These may be reminders of specific ideas or activities you can incorporate into your own repertoire. By continuing the learning process in rehearsal, you build transference of the concepts, provide direct application to your current music, and enhance the musical knowledge of all choir members.

Concept Corner

This additional information on the session's concepts can serve as a review to you in preparation for the lesson. Each idea is identified and explained in basic terms so that you know exactly how the concept works in music. It can also serve as a resource to explain the concepts to your class participants. Feel free to use your own words and examples when delivering the concepts in class. This is intended to serve as a foundation to what you will ultimately present. Consult other musical resources, as needed, to build your own working knowledge for each concept.

Whole Note   Half Note   Quarter Note

Preparation
Duplicate Worksheet 1.

Materials
Metronome

Teaching Method
1. Identify **rhythm** in everyday life.
   - Time: clock, day, month, year
   - Heartbeat

2. Identify **rhythm** in music.
   - Ordering of sound
   - Steady beat

3. Illustrate and define **rhythmic notation:** whole note, half note, quarter note.
   - Draw a quarter note.
   - Identify the note anatomy.

head →   ← stem

Quarter Note Anatomy

   - Illustrate note name/duration.

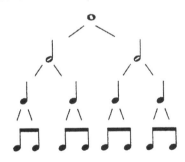

Note Name Value Chart

4. Demonstrate each note duration: whole note, half note, quarter note.
   - Clap, walk, chant, or play on an instrument.
   - Illustrate steady pulse with a metronome

5. Demonstrate the size relationship of note durations: whole note, half note, quarter note.

- Clap, chant, or play alternating note values, such as 8 quarter notes, then 4 half notes, then 2 whole notes.

Ear Training: See page 68.

Music Application: Worksheet 1

Session One worksheet includes HAMBURG. This hymn tune is often used with "When I Survey the Wondrous Cross."

In Rehearsal
- Locate examples of quarter, half, and whole notes in your choral repertoire.
- Clap and count simple rhythmic examples from the repertoire.

CONCEPT CORNER

Rhythm gives order to music and is fundamental to music making. It is the pulse that organizes beats into groups. It is the "heartbeat" of the music, bringing life and energy to the sounds.

Rhythm is defined by the shape of a note. Musicians can tell the duration or length of a note by its appearance, just as you identify your choir members by their appearance. The *whole note* is only a hollow note head—there is no stem as in all other notes. The whole note usually gets 4 beats. The *half note* is also hollow but has a stem to distinguish its appearance. The half note usually gets 2 beats. The *quarter note* has the same shape as the half note but is blackened. The quarter note usually gets 1 beat. Don't worry about the "usually." You will learn more about rhythm in the weeks to come.

Note durations are determined by the pulse of the music, but their relationship to each other never changes! A whole note is always twice as long as a half note and a half note is always twice as long as a quarter note.

Count singing allows the musician to practice pitch and rhythm at the same time. Sing the beat numbers on the melody rather than using the text. This session, you "count sing" in the worksheet hymn example.

Worksheet 1
Quarter, Half, and Whole Notes

1. Draw four examples of each note. Watch your stem direction.

2. HAMBURG

    A. Write the beats under each note.

    B. Clap and count the rhythm. (Do you see any patterns? Which lines use the same rhythm?)

    C. Count sing the rhythm.

    D. Sing the melody while tapping the quarter note pulse.

    E. What hymn text do you sing with this melody? _____

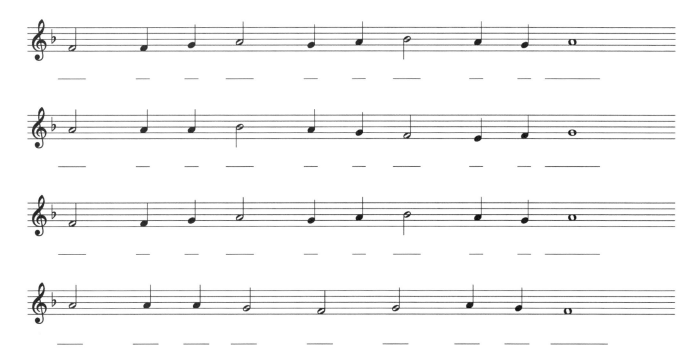

Whole Rest   Half Rest   Quarter Rest

Preparation
Duplicate Worksheet 2.

Materials
Metronome

Teaching Method
1. Review whole note, half note, quarter note.

2. Illustrate and define corresponding **rests.**
   • Notes indicate rhythmic pitch.
   • Rests indicate rhythmic silence.

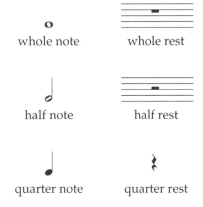

Notes/Rests Chart

3. Demonstrate each note and corresponding rest duration: whole, half, quarter.
   • Clap, chant, or play on an instrument.
   • Pull hands apart or be silent during a rest.
   • Continue counting or pulsing during the rest to indicate the appropriate rhythm.
   • Illustrate steady pulse with metronome.

Music Application: Worksheet 2
   Session Two worksheet includes sample notation (clapping rhythm patterns).

Ear Training: See page 68.

In Rehearsal
1. Locate examples of quarter, half, and whole notes/rests in your choral repertoire.

2. Clap and count simple rhythmic examples.

CONCEPT CORNER

Last week we learned that the shape of a note indicates the duration or rhythm or a pitch. Each note has a corresponding *rest,* indicating a period of silence. Rests are also identified by their shape. Rhythm, or pulses, continues through rests. It is important that musicians do not disregard rests as points of nothingness in music. Rather, the rest can add excitement, anticipation, and rhythmic clarity to even the simplest melody.

When clapping a rhythm that includes rests, pull apart the hands to distinguish silence from pitch/sound. Do maintain the pulse throughout the duration of the rests to remind your participants that the beat continues.

Notice the specific location of each rest on the staff. Both the half rest and the whole rest sit within the third space. Seeing the difference between a half rest and whole rest may challenge new music readers. Offer hints that work for you, such as the half rest looks like a hat and the whole rest looks like a hole.

Worksheet 2
Quarter, Half, and Whole Rests

1. Draw four examples of each rest.

2. Sample Notation

    A. Write the beats under each note or rest.

    B. Clap and count each rhythm example. Pull your hands apart to indicate a rest—keep counting!

    C. Count sing the rhythm on any given pitch. Count silently during rests.

    D. Clap the entire example without stopping.

    E. Clap the entire example as a round. Divide the participants into groups. You may begin the round on any beat.

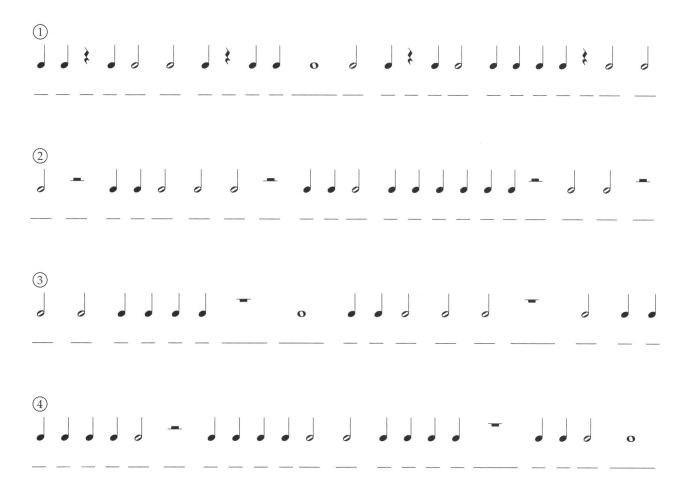

| Eighth Notes | Eighth Rest | Sixteenth Notes | Sixteenth Rest |

Preparation

1. Prepare the Note/Rest Chart. You may write this on a board or create a poster.

2. Duplicate Worksheet 3.

Materials
Metronome

Teaching Method

1. Review whole, half, quarter notes and rests.

2. Illustrate and define **eighth notes/rests** and **sixteenth notes/rests.**
   - Draw an eighth note and identify the note anatomy.

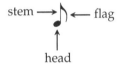

stem → ← flag

head

Eighth Note Anatomy

   - Draw a sixteenth note and identify the note anatomy.
   - Draw single examples and **beamed** examples.

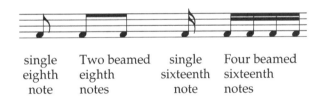

| single eighth note | Two beamed eighth notes | single sixteenth note | Four beamed sixteenth notes |

   - Illustrate eighth and sixteenth notes with rests of the same duration.

Note/Rest Chart

3. Demonstrate each note and corresponding rest duration.
   - Clap, chant, walk, or play on an instrument.
   - Illustrate steady pulse with a metronome.

Music Application: Worksheet 3
Today's worksheet includes an excerpt from Handel's "Hallelujah Chorus." This famous tune appears in his timeless oratorio, *Messiah*.

Ear Training: See page 69.

In Rehearsal

1. Identify examples of eighth and sixteenth notes/rests in your choral repertoire.

2. Refer to notes by their name and rhythmic value; encourage your choir members to do the same.

3. Clap and count simple rhythmic examples.

CONCEPT CORNER

Eighth notes and *sixteenth notes* have the same relationship as half notes and quarter notes. The eighth note/rest receives half of a beat, therefore it takes 2 eighth notes/rests to equal 1 beat. The sixteenth note/rest receives a fourth of a beat, therefore it takes 4 sixteenth notes/rests to equal 1 beat. The sixteenth is always half the length of the eighth whether it is a note indicating pitch or a rest indicating silence. You will see the relationship of note/rest lengths in the chart. Notice how each note and rest can be divided.

Notes bearing a flag, such as the eighth note and sixteenth note, may be written grouped or *beamed* together to show a complete beat. The *beam* is the same as a flag. When several flagged notes appear together they can become difficult to read. Beaming notes together quickly groups notes into complete beats, making it easier for the musician to read the rhythm.

Worksheet 3
Eighth Notes/Rests and Sixteenth Notes/Rests

1. Draw four examples of each.

2. Rhythm Exercise

    A. Write the beats under each note. The first line is completed for you.

      For ♪ ⅞ use 1 &. For ♫ use & a. (This will suffice for today's exercise.)

    B. Clap and count the rhythm.

    C. Count sing the rhythm.

    D. Sing the melody while tapping the quarter note pulse.

    E. Do you recognize this famous melody? _____

Preparation

1. Write on the board the rhythm exercise located at the end of the teaching method; omit the bar lines for now.

2. Duplicate Worksheet 4.

3. Choose several hymns in 4/4 for participants to conduct during the ear training section.

Materials

Metronome

Teaching Method

1. Illustrate and define **bar line, measure,** and **double bar line.**

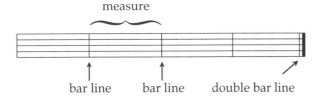

measure

bar line   bar line   double bar line

2. Illustrate and define **time signature.**
   • Write example of 4/4 **(common time).**

$\frac{4}{4}$

Time Signature

𝄴 (common time)

   • Define the role of each number and the symbol "common time."
   • Define several examples of time signatures, such as 4/4, 3/4, 12/4.

3. Illustrate how time signature defines measure length and bar line placement.
   • Display the following example on the board without bar lines.

• Guide the participants in placing bar lines in the music.
• Include a double bar line at the end of the example.
• Identify the number of measures.
• Clap and count the rhythm based on the time signature (e.g., 1-2-3-4).

Music Application: Worksheet 4

Today's worksheet includes EASTER HYMN. This hymn tune is often used with "Jesus Christ Is Risen Today."

Ear Training: See page 69.

In Rehearsal

1. Identify and define the time signature of each piece.

2. Identify measure numbers and/or rehearsal letters in the music.

3. Clap and count rhythm as part of the rehearsal learning process.

CONCEPT CORNER

Music is ordered sound. Order is achieved by pitch and rhythm. The *time signature* identifies how the beats are grouped. The top number of the time signature tells how many beats are in each measure. Each measure will contain the same number of beats. The lower number of the time signature indicates which note is equal to 1 beat. This number may change, altering the value of every note but not the relationship of the notes to each other.

Common time is another way to write 4/4 meter. The 4/4 time signature is the most "common" in music.

Bar lines are inserted at regular metric intervals, based on the time signature, to organize the notes into equal groups. The notes contained between two bar lines become a *measure*. The end of a song is identified by a double bar line.

Worksheet 4
Time Signature

EASTER HYMN

A. Write the $\frac{4}{4}$ time signature at the beginning of the first line.

B. Draw in bar lines as indicated by the time signature.

C. Draw a double bar line at the end of the hymn.

D. Write the beats in the blanks below the music.

E. Clap and count the rhythm.

F. Count sing the hymn.

G. What hymn text do you sing with this tune? _____

Preparation
Duplicate Worksheet 5.

Teaching Method
1. Draw a staff.

2. Define lines and spaces.
   • Number each line and space.
   • Always number bottom to top.

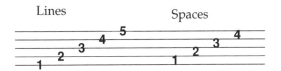

Lines   Spaces

Lines and Spaces Numbered

3. Compare the staff to a human hand.
   • Fingers represent staff lines.
   • Spaces between fingers represent staff spaces.

Staff and Human Hand

4. Identify **line** and **space** notes.

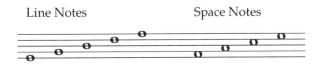

Line Notes   Space Notes

Examples of Line and Space Notes

5. Demonstrate how notes move on the staff.
   • Demonstrate notes moving up the staff (sounds higher in pitch).
   • Demonstrate notes moving down the staff (sounds lower in pitch).
   • Demonstrate repeating notes on the staff (no change in pitch).

down

up   repeat

Note Movement: Up, Down, Repeat

Music Application: Worksheet 5
Today's worksheet includes HERZLEIBSTER JESU. This hymn tune is often used with "Ah, Holy Jesus."

Ear Training: See page 69.

In Rehearsal
1. Use note movement (up, down, repeat) as part of the learning process.

2. Use a phrase from your repertoire to:
   • Identify the location of a note on the staff (e.g., line 3; space 4).
   • Identify note movement (up, down, repeat).
   • Sing the phrase as a response to this musical information.

3. Review bar line, measure, double bar line, time signature.

CONCEPT CORNER

Musical notation has evolved from no lines to the five lines/four spaces format we use today known as the *staff*. This notation was developed by Guido d'Arezzo using his own hand to identify the location of each pitch. Modify his method with your participants by using the hand as a practice staff. Turn the hand sideways to discover your own portable musical staff ready to practice pitch names.

Notes "sit" either on a *line* or in a *space*. The location of a note on the staff determines its pitch. It is important that your participants quickly recognize the location of any note.

Notes on the staff move *up, down,* or *repeat.* Quick recognition of pitch movement makes sight reading much easier. There is a direct correlation to note movement on the staff and pitch movement. Notes sound higher as they move up the staff and lower as they move down the staff.

Echo singing is a quick means to involve your participants in a concept. Play or sing an example, then have the participants sing back what they heard. Listen for complete accuracy. This helps build tonal memory, the ability to hear and reproduce music. Repeat the process, as needed, for accuracy.

Worksheet 5

Musical Staff

1. Number each line and space on the staff. Remember to number from bottom to top.

Lines   Spaces

2. Identify the location of each note on the staff. L = line note, S = space note   Example: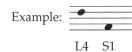

L4   S1

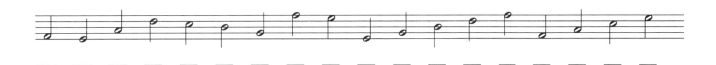

3. HERZLIEBSTER JESU

    A. Fill in the missing notes to complete the hymn.

    B. Identify note movement: up, down, repeat.

    C. Sing through the hymn.

    D. What hymn text do you sing with this tune? _____

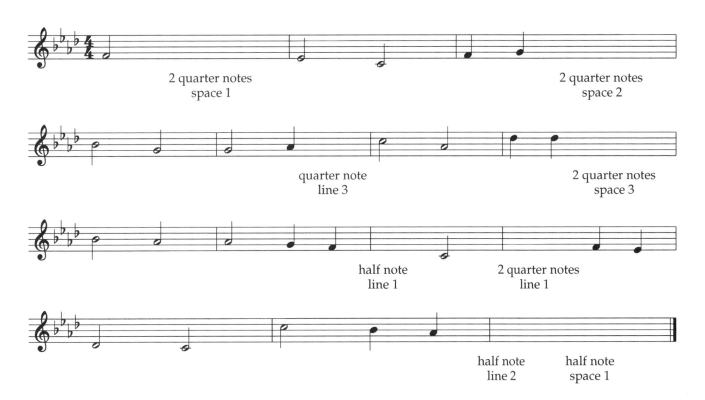

Preparation

1. Duplicate Worksheet 6.

2. Practice drawing the treble/G clef.

Materials

Step bells

Teaching Method

1. Introduce the **musical alphabet:** A B C D E F G

2. Explain how the musical alphabet moves on the staff.
   - Read forward when moving up the staff.
   - Read backward when moving down the staff.
   - The musical alphabet repeats itself regardless of the direction it is moving.

3. Introduce the **treble/G clef.**
   - Draw an example of a G clef.

Treble/G Clef and G Line Example

   - The treble clef defines the location of G line 2.
   - The shape resembles an ancient letter G.
   - Give examples of voices/instruments that use this clef.

4. Label notes common to the treble/G clef.

Note Names on Treble Clef

   - Demonstrate that the note names move in musical alphabet order.
   - Play examples on the keyboard or step bells; name the notes as you play.
   - Sing from a treble staff on note names moving up and down.

5. Demonstrate that notes can move beyond the staff.
   - Define **ledger line.**
   - Add middle C and D below the staff.
   - Add G and A above the staff.

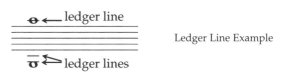

Ledger Line Example

6. Use sentences to remember note locations.
   - Treble lines: Every Good Boy Does Fine.
   - Treble spaces: FACE.

Music Application: Worksheet 6

Today's worksheet includes MORECAMBE. This hymn tune is often used with "Spirit of God, Descend Upon My Heart."

Ear Training: See page 69.

In Rehearsal

1. Locate treble/G clef in repertoire.

2. Name treble/G clef notes in a sample phrase.

3. Refer to treble/G clef notes by their name.

4. Apply concepts to a phrase requiring additional attention in rehearsal.
   - Identify the note movement (up, down, repeat).
   - Name the treble/G clef notes.
   - Sing the phrase.

CONCEPT CORNER

The *musical alphabet* uses only seven letters: A B C D E F G. The letters move in order along the staff. Movement up the staff raises the pitch; movement down the staff lowers the pitch.

The *treble/G clef* identifies the G pitch on the second line. This corresponds to the G above middle C on the piano. All other notes can be identified in relation to the G. Some who use the treble/G clef: women and children singers, violin, flute, oboe, clarinet, saxophone, and trumpet.

Tenors have a special challenge as music readers because their clef may change. The tenor line may be written in treble clef, sung one octave lower, in vocal tenor clef or octave treble clef, sung one octave lower, or in bass clef.

Ledger lines allow the staff to be expanded up and down. Small lines are added, as needed, to indicate notes outside of the five lines and four spaces of the staff.

Worksheet 6
Treble/G Clef

1. Fill in the missing letters moving left to right.

    __   B   C   __   E   __   __

2. Fill in the missing letters moving right to left.

    __   B   __   D   __   __   G

3. Draw four treble/G clefs. Trace over the G line (line 2) with a dark pencil.

4. Write the note name below each pitch.

5. MORECAMBE

    A. Write the note name below each pitch.

    B. Identify if the notes move up, down, or repeat.

    C. How many measures are in this hymn? _____

    D. Sing the note names with this hymn tune.

    E. What hymn text do you sing with this tune? _____

6. Ear Training

    A. Write the second pitch that is played.

    B. Write the name of both pitches in the blanks.

Preparation
1. Duplicate Worksheet 7.

2. Practice drawing a bass/F clef.

Materials
Step bells

Teaching Method
1. Review the musical alphabet.

2. Introduce **bass/F clef.**
   • Draw an example of a bass/F clef.

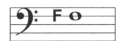

Bass/F Clef Example

   • Purpose of the clef is to identify the F line.
   • The shape resembles the letter F.
   • Give examples of voices/instruments that use this clef.

3. Label notes common to the bass clef.

E F G A B C D E F G A B middle C

Note Names on Bass Clef

4. Use sentences to remember note location.
   • Lines: Good Boys Do Fine Always.
   • Spaces: All Cows Eat Grass.

5. Demonstrate that notes move up and down the staff in musical alphabet order.

6. Play an example on the keyboard or step bells.

7. Sing from the staff on note names moving up and down.

8. Demonstrate that notes can move beyond the staff.
   • Review ledger line.
   • Add B and middle C above the staff.
   • Add F and E below the staff.

middle C D E D

Bass Clef Ledger Lines

Music Application: Worksheet
Today's worksheet includes STUTTGART. This hymn tune is often used with "Child of Blessing, Child of Promise," "Come, Thou Long-Expected Jesus," and "O My Soul, Bless God the Father."

Ear Training: See page 70.

In Rehearsal
1. Locate the bass clef in repertoire.

2. Name bass clef notes in a sample phrase.

3. Name bass clef notes in a phrase requiring additional rehearsal attention.
   • Identify pitch movement up, down, or repeat.
   • Sing the phrase.

CONCEPT CORNER

The *bass/F clef* is simply a continuation of the staff. You will notice that note names continue to move in musical alphabet order through both the treble/G clef and the bass/F clef. The clef symbol identifies the F pitch located on the fourth line. This corresponds to the first F below middle C on the piano. All other notes may be identified in relation to the F line.

Encourage participants to create their own humorous sentences to remember the names of each line and space of the bass/F clef. Some who use the bass/F clef: tenor (sometimes) and bass singers, cello, double bass, trombone, tuba, and timpani.

Worksheet 7
Bass/F Clef

1. Draw four bass/F clefs. Trace over the F line (line 4) with a dark pencil.

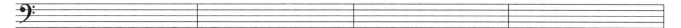

2. Write the note name below each pitch.

3. STUTTGART

    A. Write the note name below each pitch.

    B. Identify if the notes move up, down, or repeat.

    C. How many measures are in this hymn? _____

    D. Sing the note names with this hymn tune.

    E. What hymn text do you sing with this tune? _____

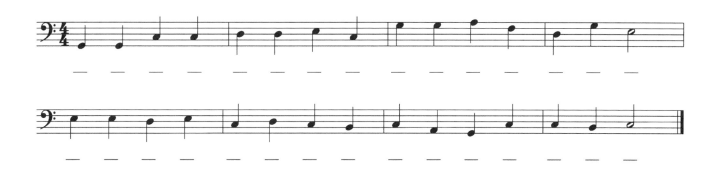

4. Ear Training

    A. Write the second pitch that is played.

    B. Write the name of both pitches in the blanks.

Preparation
Duplicate Worksheet 8.

Materials
Step bells

Teaching Method
1. Draw the grand staff and identify its parts.

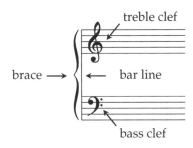

Grand Staff

2. Identify examples of grand staff use.
   • Women's and men's choral parts
   • Right hand and left hand for piano
   • Right hand, left hand (and feet) for organ

3. The grand staff may be expanded to include all the parts. (See page 79 for example.)

4. Show various musical scores with the grand staff.
   • Choral music with multiple parts and accompaniment
   • Organ
   • Orchestra or band

5. Watch for braces and bar lines to know which staves are connected.

6. Notes can move as step, skip, or repeat.
   • Movement may be up, down, or unchanged.
   • Draw examples of each.

| Step | Skip | Repeat |

Note Movement Examples: Step, Skip, Repeat

   • Play examples of each, and echo sing.

Music Application: Worksheet 8
Today's worksheet includes ADORO TE DEVOTE. This hymn tune is used with "Humbly I Adore Thee."

Ear Training: See page 70.

In Rehearsal
1. Identify the grand staff and brace groupings in your choral repertoire.
   • Note the vocal and accompaniment lines.

2. Identify steps, skips, repeats in your repertoire.

3. Use the following vocal exercises to introduce these intervalic and directional relationships.
   • Repeat each example, moving up by half steps.

Steps

Skips

Steps and Skips

CONCEPT CORNER

The *grand staff* combines staves to indicate multiple parts that move through time together. Groupings are indicated by the brace and bar line to the left of the clefs and may include vocal parts, keyboard accompaniment, or instruments. Organists may see 3 staves grouped together to indicate music for the right hand, left hand, and feet. An orchestra conductor will see all the orchestra parts grouped together in a large score.

Moving on the staff by *step* indicates the distance of one note to the adjacent note. Moving by *skip* omits the adjacent note name and skips to the next. Movement may be up or down. *Repeat* restates the same pitch.

Worksheet 8

Grand Staff

1. Complete 4 examples of the grand staff. Include brace, bar line, treble clef, and bass clef.

2. Draw the missing half note. Write the names of both notes in the blanks.

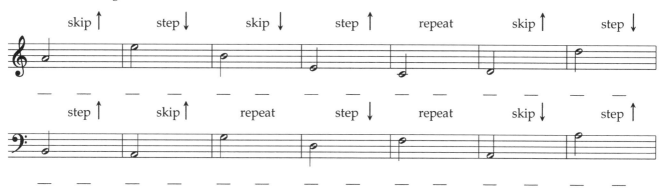

3. ADORO TE DEVOTE

   A. Circle your response above each example: step, skip, repeat.

   B. Sing the note names with this tune.

   C. What hymn text do you sing with this tune? _____

4. Ear Training

Preparation
1. Duplicate Worksheet 9.

2. Choose several hymns in 3/4 for participants to conduct during the ear training section.

Materials
Step bells

Teaching Method
1. Introduce the dotted note value.
   - A dot may be added to any note or rest.
   - A dot adds ½ of the main note's value.

2. Introduce the **dotted half note.**

$$\text{♩} + \text{♩} = \text{♩.}$$

$$(2 + 1 = 3)$$

Dotted Note Example

3. Review parts of the time signature (see Session Four).

4. Review 4/4 time signature.

5. Introduce 3/4 time signature.
   - Write the following clapping example on the board without bar lines.
   - Guide the participants in placing bar lines in the music using the time signature.
   - Include a double bar line at the end.
   - Identify the number of measures.
   - Clap and count the rhythm based on the time signature (e.g., 1-2-3).

Clapping Example

Music Application: Worksheet 9
Today's worksheet includes MARYTON. This hymn tune is often used with "O Master, Let Me Walk with Thee."

Ear Training: See pages 70-71.

In Rehearsal
1. Identify and define the time signature in each piece.

2. Review measure numbers and rehearsal letters.

3. Clap and count rhythm as part of the rehearsal learning process.

4. Look for dotted half notes in your repertoire.

CONCEPT CORNER

You learned in Session One that the shape of a note or rest determines its length/rhythm. Musicians may add a dot following any note or rest to extend the note's value by one half. The main note plus 1/2 of the note results in the new dotted note's value. The example used in today's session identifies the dotted half note.

Apply this formula: half note (2 beats) plus 1/2 of the half note (1 beat) equals 3 beats, the value of the dotted half note. This formula works for any dotted note or rest. You try it: how long is a dotted quarter note in 3/4 meter? The answer is given at the end of this section!

The 3/4 meter works much like 4/4. The quarter note still receives one beat, however, each measure contains only 3 beats. The strong-weak-weak pulse combination distinguishes this meter from 4/4. The 3/4 meter closely resembles the feeling of dancing a waltz (the 4/4 meter feels like a march).

The whole rest in 3/4 meter receives only three beats. In 4/4 meter, the whole rest receives four beats. Don't let the change confuse you. Remember that the whole rest takes up the WHOLE measure. Nothing else will fit. It makes reading the whole rest quite simple. And, the answer to the dotted quarter note in 3/4 meter is 1 1/2 beats!

Worksheet 9
¾ Meter

1. Write the count/beats in the blanks below each note/rest.

— — — — — — — — — —

2. Add one A to complete each measure.

3. MARYTON

    A. Write the **¾** time signature at the beginning of the first line.

    B. Draw in bar lines as indicated by the time signature.

    C. Draw a double bar line at the end of the hymn.

    D. Write the beats in the blanks below the music.

    E. Clap and count the rhythm.

    F. Count sing the hymn.

    G. What hymn text do you sing with this tune? _____

Preparation
Duplicate Worksheet 10.

Materials
Step bells

Teaching Method
1. Introduce intervals.
   • Discuss the distance between two notes.
   • Identify by counting the first and last notes and all lines and spaces between the notes.

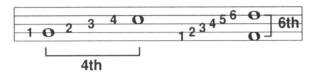

Intervals Identified

2. Intervals may be identified as melodic or harmonic.
   • Melodic intervals are performed one note at a time.

melodic 2nd   melodic 3rd

Melodic Intervals

   • Harmonic intervals are performed simultaneously.

harmonic 2nd   harmonic 3rd

Harmonic Intervals

3. Define interval: 2nd.
   • A 2nd is the same as a step.
   • Demonstrate examples of melodic and harmonic 2nd.
   • Write examples on board.
   • Play and sing examples (use step bells or piano).

4. Define interval: 3rd.
   • A 3rd is the same as a skip.
   • Demonstrate examples of melodic and harmonic 3rd.
   • Write examples on board.
   • Play and sing examples (use step bells or piano).

Music Application: Worksheet 10
Today's worksheet includes TRENTHAM. This hymn tune is often used with "Breathe On Me, Breath of God."

Ear Training: See page 72.

In Rehearsal
1. Look for 2nd and 3rd intervals in repertoire.

2. Identify both melodic and harmonic intervals.

3. Sing the melodic ear training examples as vocal exercises.
   • Identify the intervals.
   • Sing and transpose up or down by half steps.

CONCEPT CORNER

Intervals represent a musical unit of measure used to determine the distance between two pitches. An interval is identified by counting the starting note, the ending note, and any lines or spaces between the notes. Numbers are used to define the interval, such as a 2nd, 3rd, 4th, and so on. Two exceptions should be noted: a pitch that repeats itself, such as middle C and middle C, is called "unison"; a pitch that repeats itself 8 notes higher or lower, such as middle C and the next C on the staff, is called an "octave."

Melodic intervals are two pitches that occur one after the other. An easy way to remember this is to think "melody." A melody can be sung by one person, one note after the another.

Harmonic intervals are two pitches that occur simultaneously. An easy way to remember this is to think "harmony." To sing in harmony requires more than one musician sounding together.

Worksheet 10

Intervals: 2nds and 3rds

1. Draw the missing melodic interval pitch as indicated by the arrow.

2. Write the note names in the blanks.

3. Draw the missing harmonic interval pitch below the given note.

4. Write the note names in the boxes.

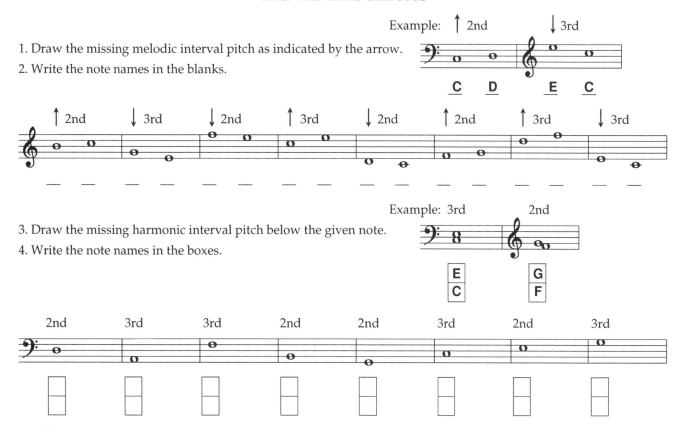

5. TRENTHAM

    A. Circle and label the following intervals: harmonic 2nd (H2) and harmonic 3rd (H3)

    B. Clap and count this hymn tune.

    C. Sing this hymn tune.

    D. What hymn text do you sing with this tune? _____

Preparation
Duplicate Worksheet 11.

Materials
Step bells (optional for interval demonstration).

Teaching Method
1. Review intervals (see Session Ten).
   • What is an interval?
   • How do we measure an interval?
   • Is the interval harmonic or melodic?

2. Define interval: 4th

melodic 4th   *harmonic 4th*

Intervals: Melodic and Harmonic 4th

• Demonstrate examples of melodic and harmonic 4th.
• Write examples on the board.
• Play and sing examples (use step bells or piano).

3. Define interval: 5th

melodic 5th   *harmonic 5th*

Intervals: Melodic and Harmonic 5th

• Demonstrate examples of melodic and harmonic 5th.
• Write examples on the board.
• Play and sing examples (use step bells or piano).

Music Application: Worksheet 11
Today's worksheet includes HURSLEY. This hymn tune is often used with "Come, Sinners, to the Gospel Feast."

Ear Training: See page 72.

In Rehearsal
1. Look for 4th and 5th intervals in repertoire.

2. Identify both melodic and harmonic intervals.

3. Sing the melodic ear training examples as vocal exercises.
   • Identify the intervals.
   • Sing and transpose up or down by half steps.

Ear Training: See page 72.

CONCEPT CORNER

Practice your own ear training skills. Music software and online sites provide opportunities for you and your choir to improve interval listening and singing skills. Consider establishing a technology corner in your music room. A computer, music software, headphones, and possibly speakers are all you need to get started. Encourage your choir members to arrive early, stay late, or visit on non-rehearsal days for extra practice. Some of your members may be willing to purchase software for home use or work with free online sites. You will notice immediate results in the reading skills of your ensemble.

Worksheet 11

Intervals: 4ths and 5ths

1. Draw the missing melodic interval pitch as indicated by the arrow.

2. Write the note names in the blanks.

3. Draw the missing harmonic interval pitch above the given note.

4. Write the note names in the boxes.

5. HURSLEY

   A. Circle and label the following intervals: harmonic 2nd (H2), 3rd (H3), 4th (H4), and 5th (H5)

   B. Clap and count this hymn tune; review $\frac{3}{4}$ meter.

   C. Sing this hymn tune.

   D. What hymn text do you sing with this tune? _____

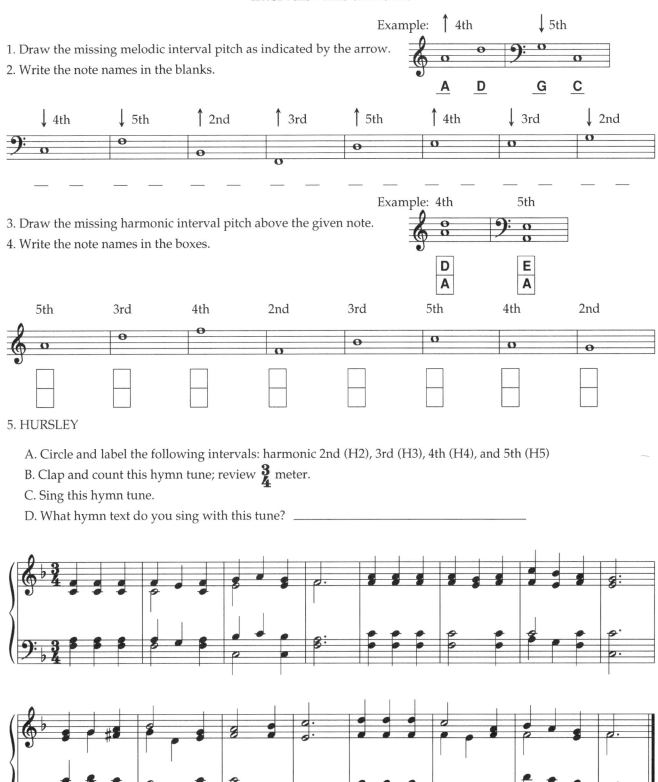

Preparation
Duplicate Worksheet 12.

Materials
Step bells (optional for interval demonstration).

Teaching Method
1. Review intervals.
   • Play and sing examples of 2nd, 3rd, 4th, and 5th.

2. Define interval: 6th
   • Demonstrate examples of melodic and harmonic 6th.
   • Write examples on the board.
   • Play and sing examples (use step bells or piano).

melodic 6th   *harmonic 6th*

Intervals: Melodic and Harmonic 6th

3. Define interval: 7th
   • Demonstrate examples of melodic and harmonic 7th.
   • Write examples on the board.
   • Play and sing examples (use step bells or piano).

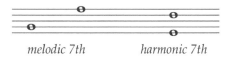

melodic 7th   *harmonic 7th*

Intervals: Melodic and Harmonic 7th

4. Define interval: octave
   • Often abbreviated as **8va.**
   • Demonstrate examples of melodic and harmonic octave.
   • Write examples on the board.
   • Play and sing examples (use step bells or piano).

Music Application: Worksheet 12
   Today's worksheet includes BEECHER. This hymn tune is often used with "Love Divine, All Loves Excelling."

melodic octave   *harmonic octave*

Intervals: Octave

Ear Training: See page 72.

In Rehearsal
1. Look for 6th, 7th, and octave intervals in repertoire.

2. Identify both melodic and harmonic intervals.

3. Sing the melodic ear training examples as vocal exercises.
   • Identify the intervals.
   • Sing and transpose up or down by half steps.

CONCEPT CORNER

   This curriculum teaches the intervals unison (a repeated pitch) through the octave. Intervals continue beyond the octave. Continue to count the distance between notes in the same manner. Once you pass the octave, the next intervals are the 9th, 10th, 11th, and so on. These intervals expand the first octave. You may notice that the 9th and 2nd are the same note name an octave apart. The 10th and 3rd are the same, as are the 11th and 4th.

Worksheet 12

Intervals: 6ths, 7ths, and 8va (octave)

1. Draw the missing melodic interval pitch as indicated by the arrow.

2. Write the note names in the blanks.

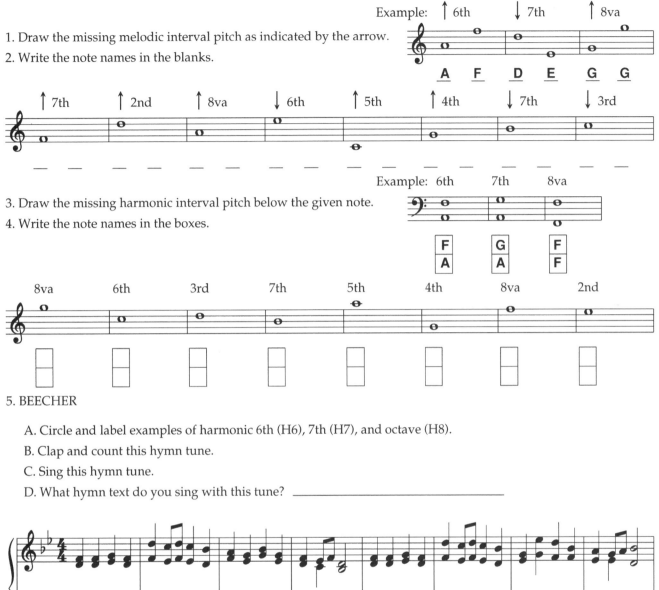

3. Draw the missing harmonic interval pitch below the given note.

4. Write the note names in the boxes.

5. BEECHER

    A. Circle and label examples of harmonic 6th (H6), 7th (H7), and octave (H8).

    B. Clap and count this hymn tune.

    C. Sing this hymn tune.

    D. What hymn text do you sing with this tune? _____

Preparation
Duplicate Worksheet 13.

Teaching Method
1. Define accidental.
   * Symbol used to alter a pitch (such as sharp, flat, natural)
   * May move a note up or down.

2. Define and demonstrate the sharp symbol.
   * Draw a sharp on a line and on a space.

Sharp Symbol, Line and Space

   * Precedes the note it changes.
   * When spoken, sharp follows the note name (such as "F sharp").
   * Must be on the same line or space as the note it alters.
   * Alters all notes by the same name that follow in the measure.
   * Raises a note a half step (sounds higher).

3. Define and demonstrate half step (semitone).
   * Smallest distance between two pitches in traditional Western music.
   * Movement from one pitch to the next closest possible pitch, up or down.

4. Define and demonstrate the natural symbol.
   * Draw a natural on a line and on a space.

Natural Symbol, Line and Space

   * Precedes the note it changes.
   * When spoken, the natural follows the note name (such as "F natural").
   * Must be on the same line or space as the note it alters.
   * Alters all notes by the same name that follow in the measure.
   * Returns the pitch to the "white key" on a piano, the unaltered note.
   * May move a note up or down.
     - √ When moving from a natural to a sharp, the pitch moves higher.
     - √ When moving from a sharp to a natural, the pitch moves lower.

Musical Application: Worksheet 13
Today's worksheet includes REST. This hymn tune is often used with "Dear Lord and Father of Mankind."

Ear Training: See page 72.

In Rehearsal
1. Look for sharps and naturals in your repertoire.

2. Extract examples of each, identifying how individual notes are altered, up or down.

3. Sing specific examples in your repertoire.

CONCEPT CORNER

An *accidental* is a symbol, such as a sharp, flat, or natural sign, that precedes a pitch to alert the musician to change the following note. The *sharp* raises the pitch by a half step. A *half step* or *semitone* is the smallest interval used in traditional Western music. For example, sing C to D. Now sing C, C♯, D. You will notice that the C♯ fits nicely between the C and D.

There are two unique half steps in music: E to F and B to C. There is no "black" key between either of these notes. They are a half step apart.

The sharp symbol must precede the note it alters in order to warn the musician. When speaking the note name, "sharp" follows the note, as in "C sharp." A sharp raises a pitch by a half step. The sharp alters all like pitches that follow in the same measure. Notes return to their original state once the measure is completed.

The *natural* symbol always moves a pitch to its unaltered state, as in the white key on a piano. A natural may move a pitch up or down depending on how it is used. When changing from a sharp to a natural, the pitch moves down. The natural sign has similar properties to the sharp as it alters all like pitches that follow in the same measure. The bar line cancels its effect with notes returning to their original state.

Worksheet 13
Sharp and Natural

1. Draw four sharps on different lines.

Draw four sharps on different spaces.

2. Draw four naturals on different lines

Draw four naturals on different spaces.

3. Add a sharp in front of each note.
4. Write the note name in the blank.

5. REST

    A. Draw a circle around each sharp.

    B. Draw a box around each natural.

    C. Write the name of each note in the blank.

    D. Sing the hymn tune.

    E. What hymn text do you sing with this tune? _____

6. Ear Training

The leader will play the first note followed by the second note.

    A. Add the appropriate accidental (♯ or ♮) to the second note.

    B. Write the names of both notes in the blanks.

SESSION FOURTEEN

Preparation
Duplicate Worksheet 14.

Teaching Method
1. Review terms from Session Thirteen.
   • Accidental
   • Sharp
   • Half step
   • Natural

2. Define and demonstrate the flat sign.
   • Draw a flat on a line and on a space.

Flat Symbol, Line and Space

   • Precedes the note it changes.
   • When spoken, flat follows the note name (such as "E flat").
   • Must be on the same line or space as the note it alters.
   • Alters all notes by the same name that follow in the measure.
   • Lowers a note a half step (sounds lower).

3. Demonstrate the natural sign in relation to the flat.
   • When moving from a natural to a flat, the pitch moves lower.
   • When moving from a flat to a natural, the pitch moves higher.

Musical Application: Worksheet 14
   Today's worksheet includes DEO GRACIAS. This hymn tune is often used with "O Love, How Deep."

Ear Training: See page 73.

In Rehearsal
1. Look for accidentals in your repertoire, especially flats.

2. Extract examples of each, noting how individual notes are altered, up or down.

3. Sing specific examples in your repertoire.

CONCEPT CORNER

The *flat* symbol must precede the note it alters in order to warn the musician. When speaking the note name, "flat" follows the note, as in "B flat." A flat lowers a pitch by a half step. The flat alters all like pitches that follow in the same measure. Notes return to their original state once the measure is completed.

Worksheet 14

Flat

1. Draw four flats on different lines. Draw four flats on different spaces.

 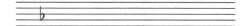

2. Add a flat in front of each note.

3. Write the note name in the blank.

4. DEO GRACIAS

    A. Draw a circle around each flat.

    B. Sing the hymn tune.

    C. What hymn text do you sing with this tune? _____

5. Ear Training

The leader will play the first note followed by the second note.

    A. Add the appropriate accidental (♭, ♯, ♮) to the second note.

    B. Write the names of both notes in the blanks.

Preparation
Duplicate Worksheet 15.

Teaching Method
1. Review sharp, flat, and natural symbols (Sessions Thirteen and Fourteen).

2. Define "enharmonic" and give examples.

C♯ D♭   F E♯

Enharmonic Examples

- One pitch may be identified by different note names.
- Note name determined by:
  - ✓ Location on the staff
  - ✓ Rules of music theory (key or harmonic relationships)
- Both note "spellings" sound identical.

3. Write these and your own examples on the board,

A♯ B♭   F♯ G♭   C B♯   B C♭   D♯ E♭

Enharmonic Writing and Playing Examples

4. Play examples on a keyboard and sing.

Music Application
Today's worksheet includes JESUS LOVES ME. The hymn tune is not identified on the worksheet so as not to influence the reading of the awkward note spellings. This enharmonic activity is designed to demonstrate the importance of note names.

Ear Training: See page 73.

In Rehearsal
1. Look for accidentals in your repertoire.

2. Continue reviewing sharp, flat, and natural signs and how they alter a given pitch.

3. Practice enharmonic spellings (ask participants to give another name for notes using accidentals).

CONCEPT CORNER

Enharmonic is the musical term allowing the same pitch to be identified by multiple names, such as C and B♯. Music theory rules govern how a note may be identified based on the key or harmonic structure. This may be troubling to the beginning musician and can bring confusion with early encounters. The use of enharmonic spelling developed from the origins of written music when these notes were actually different pitches. As instrument design and tuning became more refined, the enharmonic pitches became standardized, sharing the same tonal frequencies. This allowed musicians to play in any key on a single instrument. Today we take for granted the ability to move freely between sharps, flats, and naturals.

Worksheet 15
Enharmonic

1. Draw the enharmonic equivalent for each example. Write the name of both notes in the blanks.

__ / __   __ / __   __ / __   __ / __   __ / __   __ / __   __ / __   __ / __

2. This familiar hymn tune has been set with odd accidentals.

    A. Rewrite the hymn using the enharmonic spelling for each circled note.

    B. Sing the hymn looking at version 1.

    C. Sing the hymn looking at version 2.

    D. Which setting seems easier to read/sing? _____ Why? _____

    E. What hymn text do you sing with this tune? _____

Version 1:

Version 2:

3. Ear Training

The leader will play the given note and one other note 1/2 step up or down.

    A. Sing the example you hear played.

    B. Write the second note which is played.

    C. Write the names of both notes in the blanks. *(Note to leader: Student may write enharmonic).*

__ / __   __ / __   __ / __   __ / __   __ / __   __ / __   __ / __   __ / __

Preparation

1. Duplicate Worksheet 16.

2. Write slur examples on the board.

3. Write tie examples on the board.

Teaching Method

1. Draw examples of slurs.

Concepts: Slurs

2. Define slurs.
   - Arched line, connects two or more different pitches.
   - Indicates to sing/play **legato.**
   - May indicate a musical **phrase.**
   - In choral music, may indicate notes sung on one syllable.

Al – le – lu – ia

Choral Slur Example

3. Play and sing examples of slurs.

Slur Examples

4. Draw examples of ties.

Tie Examples

5. Define ties.
   - Arched line, connects two or more like pitches.
   - Notes must be on the same line or space.
   - Allows composer to write longer note values.

6. Play and sing examples of ties.

Play/Sing Tie Examples

Music Application

Today's worksheet includes MARTYRDOM. This hymn tune is often used with "Alas! and Did My Savior Bleed."

Ear Training: See page 73.

In Rehearsal

1. Look for slurs and ties in your repertoire.

2. Challenge your singers not to break/breathe during a slur.

3. Practice clapping and counting phrases with ties in your repertoire.

CONCEPT CORNER

Slurs and *ties* look similar. Both are arched lines but have very different musical roles. The key to telling them apart is found in the notes they connect.

Slurs connect two or more *different pitches.* The slur indicates that the notes are to be played/sung *legato,* smooth and connected. Most music is performed *legato* without any special notation. Smooth, fluid sounds are implied unless additional marks appear in the music. A composer may choose to use a slur when a single syllable of text is sung on several different notes. A slur may be used to indicate the **phrase,** a musical thought or idea. Phrases often are grouped in four or eight measures, although other lengths are possible. Sometimes phrases are very short, using only a few notes.

Ties connect two or more notes of *the same pitch,* appearing on the same line or space. This allows the composer to create longer note values. To perform a tied note, sing/play the first note and sustain it for the combined value of all notes that are tied.

Worksheet 16
Slur and Tie

1. Identify each example as a slur or a tie. Write your response in the blank.

2. Draw a slur over each measure.

3. Draw a slur under each measure.

4. Musical Math: Draw a tie in each example. Write the combined note value ($\frac{4}{4}$) in the blank.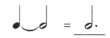

5. Note to note: Draw a tie in each example. Write an equivalent note in the blank.

6. MARTYRDOM

    A. Draw a circle around each slur.

    B. Draw a box around each tie.

    C. Clap and count the rhythm.

    D. Sing with the text. Notice how the slurs indicate a single syllable.

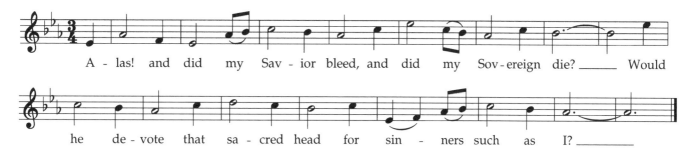

7. Ear Training: Listen for the tie(s) in each example. Write in the tie(s) you hear.

Preparation

1. Duplicate Worksheet 17.

2. Write the 6/8 meter example on the board.

3. Choose several hymns in 6/8 for participants to conduct during the ear training section.

Teaching Method

1. Review parts of a time signature.
   - Review 4/4 time signature.
   - Review 3/4 time signature.

2. Introduce 6/8 time signature.
   - Define each number in the time signature.
   - Define note values when the eighth note gets 1 beat.

3. Introduce the dotted quarter note.
   - Review dotted note values.
   - Draw and define the dotted quarter note in 4/4, 3/4, and 6/8.

$$\text{𝅗𝅥.} = 6$$
$$\text{♩.} = 3$$
$$\text{♩} = 2$$
$$\text{♪} = 1$$
$$\text{♬} = 1/2$$

Note Values in ⅜ Meter

In 4/4 and 3/4, the dotted quarter is often paired with an eighth note to complete the second beat.

Dotted Quarter /Eighth Note
in ⁴⁄₄ Meter

4. Write the following example on the board without bar lines.

⁶⁄₈ Meter Example

- Guide the participants in placing bar lines in the music using the time signature.
- Include a double bar line at the end.
- Identify the number of measures.
- Clap and count the rhythm based on the time signature and tempo; try it slow, then fast.

Note: 6/8 may be counted two ways:
- In SIX (1-2-3-4-5-6) for a slow tempo
- In TWO (1 & a 2 & a) for a fast tempo

Music Application: Worksheet 17

Today's worksheet includes IN DULCI JUBILO. This hymn tune is often used with "Good Christian Friends, Rejoice."

Ear Training: See pages 73-74.

In Rehearsal

1. Identify and define the time signature in each piece.

2. Review measure numbers and rehearsal letters.

3. Clap and count rhythm as part of the rehearsal learning process.

4. Look for dotted quarter notes in your repertoire.

CONCEPT CORNER

The 6/8 measure contains 6 beats with the eighth note getting one beat. The strong-weak-weak–strong-weak-weak pulse combination distinguishes this meter from 4/4 and 3/4. It feels as if it is rocking back and forth. The eighth notes are grouped into 2 sets of 3, making the dotted quarter the larger pulse.

The whole rest in 6/8 meter receives 6 beats. In 4/4 meter, the whole rest receives 4 beats, and in 3/4, the whole rest receives 3 beats. Don't let the change confuse you. Remember that the whole rest takes up the WHOLE measure.

You learned in Session One that the shape of a note or rest determines its length/rhythm. Session Nine introduced the dotted note/rest to extend the value by one half. The example used in today's session identifies the dotted quarter note. Remember the formula: The main note + 1/2 of the main note's value = the dotted note.

Apply this formula in 6/8 to determine the value of the dotted quarter note: quarter note (two beats) plus 1/2 of the quarter note (1 beat) equals 3 beats. This formula works for any dotted note or rest.

Worksheet 17
$\frac{6}{8}$ Meter

1. Write the beats in the blanks below each measure.

2. Add one C to complete each measure.

3. IN DULCI JUBILO

    A. Write the $\frac{6}{8}$ time signature at the beginning of the first line.

    B. Draw in bar lines as indicated by the time signature.

    C. Draw a double bar line at the end of the hymn.

    D. Write the beats in the blanks below the music.

    E. Clap and count the rhythm.

    F. Count sing the hymn.

    G. What hymn text do you sing with this tune? _____

    *Bonus: Circle the slurs; draw a box around the tie.

Preparation
Duplicate Worksheet 18.

Teaching Method
1. Draw an example of a dotted eighth note.

2. Define dotted eighth note:
   • In 6/8, receives 1 ½ beats.
   • In 4/4 or 3/4, receives ¾ beat.

3. Review sixteenth notes.
   • Draw an example of a sixteenth note.
   • Draw an example of 4 sixteenth notes beamed together.

   • Dotted eighth is often paired with a sixteenth to complete the beat.

   • Draw example of a pickup beat.

Pickup Beat

4. Define a pickup beat:
   • Included in a partial measure at the beginning of a piece.
   • The final measure is also incomplete; it must contain only the unused beats of the pickup.
   • A pickup is also referred to as an "upbeat" or "anacrusis."
   • Pickup may also refer to the note(s) immediately before a bar line, such as "the pickup to measure 17."

Note: The first complete measure of a piece is considered measure 1.

Music Application: Worksheet 18
   Today's worksheet includes GREENSLEEVES. This hymn tune is often used with "What Child Is This."

Ear Training: See page 74.

In Rehearsal
1. Identify pickup measures in your repertoire.

2. Use the term "pickup" in locating a phrase, such as the "pickup to measure 10."

3. Look for dotted eighth-sixteenth note combinations in your repertoire.

4. Reinforce rhythm, counting, and accuracy.

CONCEPT CORNER

   The *dotted eighth note* uses the same formula as all previous dotted notes: the main note + 1/2 of the main note's value = dotted note.

   The sixteenth note is usually combined with the dotted eighth to complete the beat. This pairing creates a pleasant lilt to music. It is sometimes used when swing eighths, uneven eighth notes as in jazz music, are implied. You will see this in music from the Sunday School movement of the late nineteenth and early twentieth centuries. Dotted eighth-sixteenth notes may be performed crisply, as in a march, or swinging, as in jazz. The style of music and era will help determine its proper performance.

   The pickup, upbeat, and anacrusis are all one and the same—three musical terms to describe the note(s) immediately prior to the bar line. These notes are most often connected to the phrase that continues across the bar line into the next measure. When a pickup occurs at the beginning of a piece, the final measure of the music must contain only the unused beats, so it will also be incomplete. Together these two partial measures form a complete measure.

Worksheet 18
Dotted Eighth/Sixteenth and Pickup

1. Draw four examples of ♪. ♪ in the measures.

2. Pick-up: Write the beats under each example. Watch the time signature.

3. GREENSLEEVES

    A. Draw a box around the pickup measure.

    B. Circle each ♪. ♪

    C. Write the beats in the blanks.

    D. How many beats are in the final measure? _____ Why? _____

    E. Write the name of each sharped note.

    F. Clap and count the rhythm.

    G. Sing.

4. Ear Training: Each example is one measure in 6/8.

Preparation

1. Duplicate Worksheet 19.

2. Write the 2/2 meter example on the board as described in the teaching method.

3. Choose several hymns in 2/2 for participants to conduct during the ear training section.

Teaching Method

1. Review parts of a time signature.

2. Review time signatures.

$\frac{4}{4}$ Strong-weak-strong-weak (feels like a march).

$\frac{3}{4}$ Strong-weak-weak (feels like a waltz).

$\frac{6}{8}$ Strong-weak-weak-strong-weak-weak. Feels like rocking; a sense of two strong beats divided into three smaller beats.

3. Introduce 2/2 time signature (¢ cut time).
   • Define each number in the time signature.
   • Define the symbol for cut time.
   • Note its relationship to common time. ℂ
   • Define note values when the half note gets one beat.

$$\mathbf{o} \; = \; 2$$
$$\boldsymbol{\mathralf} \; = \; 1$$
$$\boldsymbol{\flat} \; = \; 1/2$$

Note Values in $\frac{2}{2}$ Meter

4. Write the following rhythm exercise on the board without bar lines.

$\frac{2}{2}$ Rhythm Exercise

• Guide the participants in placing bar lines in the music using the time signature.
   • Include a double bar line at the end.
   • Identify the number of measures.
   • Clap and count the rhythm based on the time signature.

Music Application: Worksheet 19

Today's worksheet includes DUKE STREET. This hymn tune is often used with "From All That Dwell Below the Skies," "Jesus Shall Reign," "Forth in Thy Name, O Lord," and "I Know that My Redeemer Lives."

Ear Training: See page 74.

In Rehearsal

1. Identify and define the time signature in each piece.

2. Clap and count rhythm as part of the rehearsal learning process.

CONCEPT CORNER

The 2/2 (cut time) measure contains 2 beats with the half note getting 1 beat. The strong-weak pulse combination distinguishes this meter from 6/8 and 3/4. The cut time symbol ¢ is achieved by slicing the common time symbol ℂ in half.

The same holds true to the time signature. To create 2/2 meter, 4/4 is literally cut in half. Both 2/2 and 4/4 are interchangeable regarding the counting of the beats. However, the feel is different. The natural stresses (strong beats) in 2/2 use the half note pulse, whereas in 4/4, the stress falls on the quarter note pulse. It is a subtle difference and can be quite effective in how the music and text are interpreted.

Worshseet 19

²⁄₂ Meter, Cut Time

1. Write the beats in the blanks below each note/rest.

2. Choose the correct time signature for each example: ²⁄₂ ³⁄₄ or ⁶⁄₈

    A. Write your answer (time signature) on each example.

    B. Write the beats in the blanks below each measure.

3. DUKE STREET

    A. Draw in bar lines are indicated by the time signature.

    B. Draw a double bar line at the end of the hymn.

    C. Write the beats in the blanks below the music.

    D. Clap and count the rhythm.

    E. Count sing the hymn.

    F. What hymn text do you sing with this tune? _____

    *Bonus: Circle the slurs.

Preparation

1. Duplicate Worksheet 20.

2. Write the Triplet Rhythm Exercise on the board.

3. Look for a hymn or song from your own music tradition that uses triplets.

Teaching Method

1. Review the parts of a time signature.

2. Review 2/2 meter.

3. Review note values when the half note receives 1 beat.

4. Introduce 4/2 meter.
   - Each measure has 4 beats.
   - Half note receives 1 beat.

5. Introduce the triplet.

Eighth Note Triplet   Quarter Note Triplet

   - 3 notes replacing 2 notes of the same kind.
   - Indicated with a "3" and usually a slur.
   - Count as either:
     1-trip-let 2-trip-let
     tri-pl-et tri-pl-et

6. Triplet rhythm exercise:
   - Clap and count the Triplet Rhythm Exercise.
   - Leader claps pulse as determined by the time signature (quarter or half).
   - Participants clap the exercise.
   - Repeat as needed to secure the concept.

Music Application

Today's worksheet includes EBENEZER. This hymn tune is often used with "God Hath Spoken By the Prophets," "Let My People Seek Their Freedom," and "Once to Every Man and Nation."

Triplet Rhythm Exercise

Ear Training: See page 75

In Rehearsal

1. Introducte a hymn or song that includes triplets.

2. Look for use of triplets in your repertoire.

CONCEPT CORNER

Today's meter, 4/2, is an elongated version of cut time from Session Nineteen. Each measure contains 4 beats, with the half note getting 1 beat. The result feels very similar to 4/4 or common time, however the note values look different.

The *triplet* places 3 notes where 2 notes of the same kind "normally" fit. For example, an eighth note triplet rhythmically fits where 2 eighth notes typically fit. A quarter note triplet rhythmically fits where 2 quarter notes typically fit. This pattern is an exciting tool for composers to alter how the music "feels." It is critical to maintain a steady beat when performing triplets so that each note receives equal length. Inexperienced musicians tend to rush through the beginning of a triplet making the final note of the set too long. Practicing with a metronome or other steady pulse will help settle the rhythm.

Worksheet 20

Triplet

1. Turn these quarter notes into eighth note triplets.

2. Turn these quarter notes into quarter note triplets.

3. EBENEZER

    A. Draw in bar lines. Remember: the quarter triplets receive one beat in $\frac{4}{2}$ meter.

    B. Draw a double bar line at the end of the hymn.

    C. Write the beats in the blanks.

    D. Clap and count the rhythm.

    E. Count sing the hymn.

    F. What hymn text do you sing with this tune? _____

    *Bonus: Which three lines of this hymn are identical? _____

        How does this information help you as a musician? _____

Preparation

1. Duplicate Worksheet 21.

2. Write the dynamic examples from the teaching method on the board or create a poster chart.

Teaching Method

1. Define the term "dynamics."
   - Includes terms (most often in Italian), abbreviations, and symbols.
   - Appear within the music.
   - Identifies degree of loudness/softness.

2. Write the dynamics examples on the board.
   - Define.
   - Demonstrate.

   pp   pianissimo - very soft

   p   piano - soft

   mp   mezzo piano - moderately soft

   mf   mezzo forte - moderately loud

   f   forte - loud

   ff   fortissimo - very loud

   ◁   crescendo (cresc.) - gradually louder

   ▷   dimenuendo (dim.) - gradually softer

   Dynamics Examples

3. Experience singing dynamics.
   - Sing the scale pattern in the following exercise.
   - Vary the dynamics each time you sing.

1 2 3 4   5 6 7 8   7 6 5 4   3 2 1

Dynamic Scale Exercise

For example:
   ♫ Sing *forte* (loud)
   ♫ Sing *piano* (soft)
   ♫ Sing *mezzoforte* (moderately loud)
   ♫ Sing with an ascending crescendo and a descending diminuendo
   ♫ Sing with an ascending diminuendo and a descending crescendo

Music Application

Today's worksheet includes STEAL AWAY. The African American tune and text date back to the time of slavery. The text contains double meanings referencing both the desire to travel north for freedom and God's judgment.

Ear Training: See page 75.

In Rehearsal

1. Use the Dynamic Scale Exercise from the Teaching Method section as a vocal exercise.

2. Look for dynamics in your repertoire: define, demonstrate, and apply.

CONCEPT CORNER

Dynamics are words, abbreviations, and symbols used to describe degrees of loud and soft. Dynamics bring variety and interest to music. Composers often use dynamics to highlight text, bring drama into a section, or alter how we experience a repeated passage. It is important to look for dynamics within the music during rehearsal. These must be practiced along with notes and rhythm. Generally speaking, it is easier to control a crescendo than a diminuendo, as performers tend to become too quiet very quickly. You will improve your ensemble's sound by practicing control of both the crescendo and diminuendo.

Worksheet 21
Dynamics

1. Arrange these dynamic abbreviations from soft to loud: *mf* *p* *pp* *f* *mp* *ff*

2. Match the Italian dynamic in Column A with the English in Column B.

Column A	Column B
piano	moderately soft
mezzo forte	loud
forte	very soft
mezzo piano	soft
pianissimo	very loud
fortissimo	moderately loud

3. STEAL AWAY

   A. Circle the dynamics.

   B. Write the beats in the blanks.

   C. Clap and count the rhythm. Repeat incorporating the dynamics.

   D. Count sing the rhythm incorporating the dynamics.

   E. Sing on text incorporating the dynamics.

   *Bonus: Circle the triplets.

49

Preparation
1. Duplicate the Articulation Chart (see page 79).

2. Duplicate Worksheet 22.

Teaching Method
1. Define **articulation**.
   - Notations are near the notehead.
   - Indicates how the note is performed.

2. Distribute the Articulation Chart.

Staccato
1. Draw an example.

2. Define staccato.
   - Articulation of duration (release)
   - Sing/play note without sustaining the sound
   - Separated, detached sound

3. Demonstrate.
   - Play Ex. 22.1 (see page 79).
   - Compare *legato* and *staccato*.

Fermata
1. Draw an example.

2. Define fermata.
   - Articulation of duration.
   - Sustains the sound beyond the given note value.
   - Duration is decided by the conductor or solo performer.

3. Demonstrate.
   - Play Ex. 22.2 (see page 79).
   - Compare with the staccato example.

Tenuto
1. Draw an example.

2. Define tenuto.
   - Articulation of duration and dynamics.
   - To give note its full value.
   - To sing/play the note slightly louder than others (not as loud as an accent).

3. Demonstrate.
   - Play Ex. 22.3 (see page 79).
   - Compare with *staccato* and *fermata*.

Accent
1. Draw an example.

2. Define accent.
   - Articulation of dynamics.
   - Indicates to sing/play the note louder.

3. Demonstrate.
   - Play Ex. 22.4 (see page 79).
   - Compare with staccato, fermata, and tenuto.

Music Application: Worksheet 22
Today's worksheet uses excerpts from four hymn tunes: (1) AMEN, AMEN is used with the African American spiritual by the same name; (2) THOMPSON is known with the text "Softly and Tenderly Jesus Is Calling"; (3) UNSER HERRSCHER is often used with "God of Love and God of Power" and "He Is Risen"; and (4) DARWALL'S 148th is often used with "Rejoice, the Lord Is King" and "Break, Day of God."

Ear Training: See page 75.

In Rehearsal
1. Look for articulations symbols in your repertoire, such as slur, staccato, fermata, tenuto, or accent.

2. Identify, define, and demonstrate the articulation.

3. Teach your singers how to apply the articulation.

CONCEPT CORNER

Articulation is a means to enhance a note or group of notes. The articulation is often designated by a symbol near the notehead. These techniques allow the composer to let notes speak uniquely. Emphasis may be needed for drama, character, text description, variety in sound, or to identify the melodic notes amid a flurry of accompanying pitches.

Staccato is an articulation of duration in which the note is detached from the following note. Sing or play the note without sustaining the sound.

The *fermata* is an articulation of duration in which the length of the note is sustained beyond the note's value. The music influences the length based on the style, phrase, mood, or tempo.

Tenuto is an articulation of duration and dynamics. It may indicate to give a note its full value or to sing or play a note slightly louder than others.

An *accent* is an articulation of dynamics, indicating to sing or play the note louder. This is effective at dramatic moments or for special emphasis.

Worksheet 22

Articulation

1. Draw the designated articulation above or below each note. *(Note: The fermata is usually above the staff.)*

2. Hymn excerpts demonstrate the four articulation signs in this lesson.
   - A. Circle the articulation signs used in each example, such as the staccato marks in the first line.
   - B. Speak each example using the articulation indicated.
   - C. Sing each example using the articulation indicated.

Staccato

AMEN, AMEN

A – men, a – men, a – men, a – men, a – men!

Fermata

THOMPSON

Come home, come home; you who are wea-ry, come home;

earn-est-ly, ten-der-ly, Je-sus is call-ing, call-ing, O sin-ner come home!

Tenuto

UNSER HERRSCHER

God of love and God of power, thou hast called us for this hour.

Accent

DARWALL'S 148th

Lift up your heart, lift up your voice; re-joice; a-gain I say, re-joice.

3. Ear Training: Add the appropriate articulation(s) to each example—staccato, fermata, tenuto, or accent.

Preparation
Duplicate Worksheet 23.

Teaching Method
1. Introduce repeat and endings.
   - Musical road map signs / symbols.
   - Simplify reading by reusing music.
   - Function as musical street signs, giving directions on where to go within the music.

2. Draw a repeat sign.
   - Two dots placed before a double bar

3. Define the use of a single repeat sign.
   - Indicates to return to the beginning and "repeat" or resing/replay the music.

4. Draw a pair of repeat signs.

5. Define the use of a pair of repeat signs.
   - Indicates an internal repeat.
   - Sing/play to the repeat sign; return to the facing repeat and sing/play ONLY that section again before continuing.

6. Draw first and second endings.

7. Define the use of endings.
   - Sing to the repeat sign contained within the first ending.
   - Repeat as indicated: to the beginning of the piece or to the internal repeat sign.
   - Second time through, omit the first ending, sing the second ending and continue as indicated.

Music Application: Worksheet 23
   Today's worksheet includes excerpts from two hymns: IN DIR IST FREUDE is often used with "In Thee Is Gladness"; WORDS OF LIFE is used with "Wonderful Words of Life."

Ear Training: See page 76.

In Rehearsal
1. Look for musical road map signs and symbols, such as repeat signs and endings.

2. Define each symbol and discuss where to go in the musical score.

CONCEPT CORNER

   Musical street signs, such as the *repeat* and *endings*, simplify reading by reusing music you have already sung. Musicians recognize familiar phrases, reducing the amount of practice time needed to learn new songs. It is important to look through music before singing to discover any directional signs to avoid surprises while performing.
   The *repeat* sign is a double bar with two dots. This indicates to return to the beginning and sing/play the music again.
   Paired *repeat* signs face each other, indicating that only a section of music is to be performed again. Sing/play until the repeat sign faces back, return to its mate, which faces forward, and continue. Repeat that section only once unless the composer indicates otherwise.
   Endings allow the composer to reuse a section of music but change the final measure(s). This also saves space and paper for publishers. Any number of endings may be used; however, *first* and *second* endings are most commonly seen. Sing/play through the first ending, which always contains a repeat sign. Return, as indicated, and sing/play again. This time, omit the first ending, "jumping" to the second ending, and continuing in the music.

Worksheet 23
Repeats, First and Second Endings

1. Rewrite the following example using a repeat sign.

   Hint: Look for a measure containing music you have seen. Then, compare the
   music following to determine if a repeat sign may be used.

IN DIR IST FREUDE

In thee is glad - ness, a - mid all sad - ness, Je - sus, sun - shine of my heart.

By thee are giv - en the gifts of heav - en, thou the true Re - deem - er art.

2. First and second endings are used in the following example.

   Rewrite this hymn refrain in full, as you would sing it, without the endings.

   What is the total number of measures in this refrain? _____

WORDS OF LIFE

Beau - ti - ful words, won - der - ful words, Won - der - ful words of Life. Life.

3. Ear Training

A. Listen as the following example is played. Draw the missing repeat sign.

B. Listen as the following example is played. Draw the missing first and second endings.

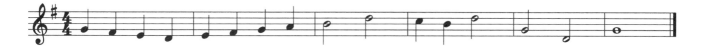

Preparation
1. Duplicate the Music Road Map Guide (page 80).

2. Duplicate Worksheet 24.

Teaching Method
1. Distribute the Music Road Map Guide.

2. Introduce D.C., D.S., fine, and coda.
   - Musical road map signs / symbols.
   - Simplify reading by reusing music.

3. Define D.C.
   - Abbreviation for *da capo* ("dah kah-poh").
   - Usually appears at the end of the printed music, indicates to return to the beginning and sing/play again, often paired with *al fine.*

4. Define *fine.*
   - Indicates the end of the piece ("FEE-neh").
   - Appears in music as *fine,* paired with a double bar line.
   - *Al fine* means "to the end": indicates to play the piece from the beginning *(D.C.)* or from the sign *(D.S.)* to the *fine* marked in the music.

5. Demonstrate *D.C. al fine.*
   - Identify directions on the Music Road Map Guide.
   - Speak the text following the *D.C. al fine.*
   - Sing the hymn with text following the *D.C. al fine.*

6. Define D.S. 𝄋
   - Abbreveiation for *dal segno* ("dal Sehn-yoh").
   - Indicates to return to the sign 𝄋 and continue
   - Often paired with *al fine* or *al coda.*

7. Define coda. ⊕
   - A closing section
   - *Al coda* means "to the coda."
   - Indicates to play from the beginning *(D.C.)* or from the sign *(D.S.)* to the coda sign. ⊕
   - Jump from the coda sign to the coda section and continue.

8. Demonstrate *D.S. al coda.*
   - Identify directions on the Music Road Map Guide.
   - Speak the text following the *D.S. al coda.*
   - Sing the hymn with text following the *D.S. al coda.*

9. D.C. and D.S. may be paired with:
   - *al fine*
   - *al coda*

Music Application: Worksheet 24
Today's worksheet includes ST. THEODULPH. This hymn tune is commonly used with "All Glory, Laud, and Honor" and "Blest Be the King Whose Coming."

Ear Training: See page 76.

In Rehearsal
1. Look for musical road map signs, such as *D.C., D.S., fine, coda,* repeat signs, and endings.

2. Define each symbol and discuss where to go in the musical score.

CONCEPT CORNER

Composers use musical street signs, such as **D.C., D.S., fine**, and **coda** to maximize print space and to simplify reading by reusing music. They may use any combination of symbols to navigate the performer through the music. It is important to look through music before singing to discover any directional signs to avoid surprises while performing.

Today's terms are Italian words commonly used in music. **D.C., da capo**, usually appears at or near the end of the printed page indicating to return to the beginning and continue.

D.S., dal segno, usually appears at or near the end of the printed page indicating to return to the sign and continue.

Fine indicates the end of the piece. It is followed by a double bar, another indication that the piece is finished. A **D.C.** or **D.S.** may be paired with **al fine**, to the end. Sing through the entire piece following all musical directions.

Coda indicates a closing section. A **D.C.** or **D.S.** may be paired with **al coda**. Sing through the entire piece following all musical directions. Observe the "to coda" instructions only on the final time through the section. Jump to the **coda** and continue.

Worksheet 24
D.C. and D.S.

1. Draw a line from each term in Column A to the appropriate definition in Column B.

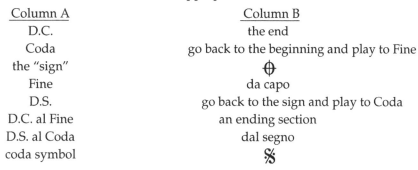

Column A	Column B
D.C.	the end
Coda	go back to the beginning and play to Fine
the "sign"	⊕
Fine	da capo
D.S.	go back to the sign and play to Coda
D.C. al Fine	an ending section
D.S. al Coda	dal segno
coda symbol	𝄋

2. ST. THEODULPH

A. Circle the time signature.

B. This hymn begins on what beat? _____

C. The first not of the refrain is called a(n) _____

   (its musical function, not the note name)

D. What is the last word sung in the hymn? _____

E. What is the first word sung after the D.C.? _____

F. How many times is the refrain sung? _____

G. How many measures are in the refrain? _____

   (Hint: measure one begins on "glory")

H. Name and define the symbol ♮ used in

   measures 9, 10, and 11. _____

I. Clap and count the rhythm.

J. Count sing the melody (or parts).

K. Sing the hymn on text.

All Glory, Laud, and Honor

Preparation
1. Write the Tempo Rhythm Example on the board.

2. Duplicate Worksheet 25.

Teaching Method
1. Define tempo marks.
   - Italian words or phrases.
   - Indicates the suggested rate of speed for a piece or section of music.
   - The general tempo of the piece appears above the first measure and may be used as the title of a piece when no other title is provided (especially common in symphonic and solo instrumental movements).

2. Intoduce the Tempo Rhythm Example.
   - Clap and count the exercise.

Tempo Rhythm Example

3. Use the exercise to demonstrate each of the following tempo marks.
   - Define each tempo mark.
   - Demonstrate each tempo by clapping the Tempo Rhythm Example at that speed.

   Largo — very slow, broad
   Adagio — slow
   Andante — moderately slow, walking tempo
   Moderato — moderately
   Allegro — fast
   Vivace — lively

4. Examples of changes in tempo:
   - Leader writes one tempo change at a time in the Tempo Rhythm Example.
   - Demonstrate each change by clapping the example.

   Ritardando (*rit.* or *ritard.*) — gradually slower
   Rallentando (*rall.*) — gradually slower
   Accelerando (*accel.*) — gradually faster
   a tempo — return to normal speed; used after an alteration in tempo
   Rubato — freely, a flexible tempo

5. More Italian terms:

   Più — more, as in *più allegro* (faster)
   Meno — less, as in *meno mosso* (less agitated)
   Molto — much, as in *molto rallentando* (much slowing)
   Poco — little, as in *poco ritardando* (little slowing)

Music Application: Worksheet 25
Today's worksheet includes HYMN TO JOY. This hymn tune is commonly used with "Joyful, Joyful, We Adore Thee" and "Sing with All the Saints in Glory."

Ear Training: See page 77.

In Rehearsal
1. Look for tempo marks at beginning of music; identify, define, demonstrate, and apply.

2. Look for tempo changes within the music; identify, define, demonstrate, and apply.

CONCEPT CORNER

Tempo marks are used by composers to aid the performer in determining the speed of the piece. Tempos vary based on the mood, character, nature of text, and technical demands of the music. You should never sacrifice accuracy for speed when performing. Tempos are relative with no set speed required. Practice at a reasonable speed for your skill level. Then, apply the tempo suggested by the composer, moving faster or slower, to achieve the desired results.

Tempo marks are usually Italian words. Consult a music dictionary for unfamiliar terms and other musical words.

Tempo changes are used for variety and dramatic effect, drawing attention to the text and helping to illustrate the meaning of a phrase. Always look for tempo identification before you begin a piece. Anticipate the desires of the composer and look for the reason behind any changes. This will help you convey the meaning of the text to your audience.

Worksheet 25

Tempo Marks

1. Arrange the following tempo marks from slowest to fastest.

   Moderato   Adagio   Allegro   Vivace   Largo   Andante

2. Define each tempo mark. Write the correct definition number in the blank beside each term.

   _____ Allegro   1. moderately slow, walking tempo

   _____ Moderato   2. very slow, broad

   _____ Andante   3. fast

   _____ Largo   4. slow

   _____ Vivace   5. moderately

   _____ Adagio   6. lively

3. Define each tempo change. Write the correct definition number in the blank beside each term.

   _____ accelerando   1. freely, flexible tempo

   _____ rubato   2. gradually slower

   _____ a tempo   3. gradually faster

   _____ rallentando   4. return to normal speed

4. Be the composer. Add the following items to the hymn. Sing your version!
   - A. Select a tempo mark and write it above the first measure.
   - B. Select a tempo change and write it somewhere within the body of the hymn.
   - C. Write "a tempo" shortly after the previous tempo change.
   - D. Write "rall." (rallentando) near the end.

   *Bonus: Share your version with other participants.

HYMN TO JOY

Joy - ful, joy - ful, we a - dore thee, God of glo - ry, Lord of love; hearts un - fold like flowers be - fore thee

o - pening to the sun a - bove. Melt the clouds of sin and sad - ness; drive the dark of

doubt a - way. Giv - er of im - mor - tal glad - ness, fill us with the light of day!

CONCEPT: Major Scale, Tetrachord, Key Note

Preparation
1. Duplicate Worksheet 26.

2. Write a C major scale on the board.

Materials Needed
Step bells

Teaching Method
1. Demonstrate the C major scale.
   - Play the scale on a keyboard or step bells.
   - Sing the scale on note letter names.
   - Sing the scale on numbers (1, 2, 3, 4, 5, 6, 7, 1).

C Major Scale

2. Define the major scale.
   - Series of eight notes in alphabetical order.
   - Contains two **tetrachords** (whole step, whole step, half step) joined by a whole step.

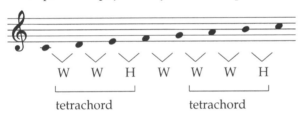

Major Scale Pattern with Tetrachord

   - Each note in the scale is numbered (scale degrees) based on its placement.

Scale Degrees

   - A scale may begin on any note.
   - There are twelve major scales, one for each note.
   - The key note gives the scale its name (key note C = C scale).

3. Practice creating a major scale.
   - Select any note as the key note (beginning and ending note of the scale).

- Apply the rules:
   - ✓ Eight notes in alphabetical order
   - ✓ Pattern: (key note) W W H W W W H
   For example:

   ① Keynote = G
   ② Apply pattern: W W H W W W H

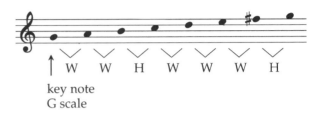

key note
G scale

Major Scale Pattern

Music Application: Worksheet 26
Today's worksheet includes ANTIOCH. This hymn tune is commonly used with "Joy to the World."

Ear Training: See page 77.

In Rehearsal
1. Sing major scales on numbers (1, 2, 3, 4, 5, 6, 7, 1) as a vocal warm-up.

2. Look for scale patterns in your music.

CONCEPT CORNER

The *major scale* is an ordering of ascending notes in a specific pattern of whole and half steps. This pattern consists of two *tetrachords*, a set of four notes arranged as (key note) W W H. The two tetrachords are linked by a whole step to create the final pattern of the major scale: (key note) W W H W W W H.

A major scale contains eight notes in alphabetical order. No letter may be omitted or repeated. Each note is a *scale degree*, or number, within the scale. The scale degree is determined by its location. Therefore, the first note is scale degree 1; the second note is scale degree 2, and so forth.

The *key note* is the first and last note of the scale. The key note gives the scale its name. Therefore, a scale beginning on C is the C scale.

Worksheet 26
Major Scale

1. The pattern for a major scale is (key note) W W H W W W H.

    A. Create a major scale starting on D.

    B. Label the key note and intervals (whole and half steps).

    C. Label the scale degrees (1, 2, 3, …).

2. Each scale has one mistake.

    A. Circle the mistake.

    B. Write the correct note in its place.

3. ANTIOCH

    A. The melody of this hymn contains a complete descending scale. Locate and circle the scale.

    B. Two partial descending scales are also used in the melody. Locate and circle these.

    C. What is the leter name of this scale? _____

    D. Clap and count the rhythm.

    E. The scale degrees are listed below each note. Sing this familiar hymn tune on scale numbers.

    F. What text do you sing with this tune? _____

    *Bonus: An octave leap is used in this melody. Find it and draw a box around it.

Preparation

1. Duplicate Worksheet 27.

2. Write the sample key signature on the board.

Teaching Method

1. Introduce key signature.
   - Set of sharps or flats (or nothing as in the key of C) appearing at beginning of each line of music following the clef.
   - Either all sharps or all flats.
   - Defines the key.
   - Indicates which notes are sharp or flat throughout the piece.

2. Define sharp order.
   - Sharps in a key signature appear in a specific order: F♯ C♯ G♯ D♯ A♯ E♯ B♯.
   - A key signature with two sharps must be F♯ and C♯.
   - Sharps in a key signature must appear on specific lines and spaces.

F C G D A E B

3. Introduce sharp key signatures.
   - Draw a grand staff on the board.
   - Add an F♯ as the key signature.
   - Identify key: G major.
   - Continue adding sharps and identifying the key signature.

G Major (F♯)

| G major | D major | A major | E major |

| B major | F♯ major | C♯ major |

Sharp Key Signatures

4. Demonstrate short-cut for naming sharp keys.
   - Key name is a half step higher than final sharp in the key signature.
   - For example: Key signature has two sharps, F♯ and C♯, the final sharp is C♯, a half step higher than C♯ is D, the name of the key (scale) is D.

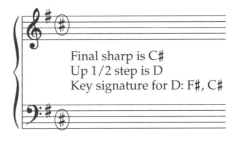

Final sharp is C♯
Up 1/2 step is D
Key signature for D: F♯, C♯

Naming Sharp Key Signature Short-cut

Music Application: Worksheet 27

Today's worksheet includes BRADBURY. This hymn tune is commonly used with "Savior, Like a Shepherd Lead Us."

Ear Training: See page 77.

In Rehearsal

1. Identify sharp key signatures used in your music.

2. Review sharp order.

CONCEPT CORNER

The *key signature* appears at the beginning of each line of music following the clef. It identifies the key used in the piece. This tonal relationship of notes contains either all sharps or all flats. The exception is C major, which has no sharps or flats. The sharps or flats of the key signature alter all notes by the same name. A key signature of two sharps (F♯ and C♯) indicates that all F's and C's are sharp throughout the piece.

Sharps used in a key signature appear in a predetermined order. *Sharp order* requires sharps to be used as: F♯ C♯ G♯ D♯ A♯ E♯ B♯.

Sharp key signatures may be identified via the final sharp in the key. Name the final sharp then go up a half step for the name of the key. For example, a key signature with five sharps (F♯ C♯ G♯ D♯ A♯) ends with A♯. Up a half step is B, the name of the key.

Worksheet 27
Sharp Key Signatures

1. Copy the sharp order three times.

2. Name the following key signatures.
   (Hint: The key is 1/2 step higher than the last sharp.)

__   __   __   __

3. Create the following key signatures.

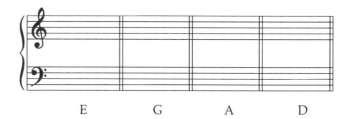

E   G   A   D

4. BRADBURY

   A. Circle the key signature.

   B. Name the key. _____

   C. Circle all F♯ and C♯ in the music.

   D. Clap and count the rhythm.

   E. Sing on scale numbers.

   F. Sing on text.

   *Bonus: Which two lines sound identical? _____

   *Bonus: What musical symbol is used three measures from the end? _____

Preparation

1. Duplicate Worksheet 28.

2. Write the sample key signature on the board.

Teaching Method

1. Review key signature.

2. Review sharp order.

3. Define flat order.

B E A D G C F

- Flats in a key signature appear in a specific order: Bb Eb Ab Db Gb Cb Fb
- A key signature with three flats must be Bb, Eb, and Ab.
- Flats in a key signature must appear on specific lines and spaces.

4. Introduce flat key signatures.

F Major (Bb)

- Draw a grand staff on the board.
- Add a Bb as the key signature.
- Identify key: F major
- Continue adding flats and identifying the key signature.

| F major | Bb major | Eb major | Ab major |

| Db major | Gb major | Cb major |

Flat Key Signatures

5. Demonstrate short-cut for naming flat keys.
- Key signature name is the next-to-last flat.
- A key signature with five flats, Bb Eb Ab Db Gb— the next-to-last flat is Db, the name of the key is Db major.

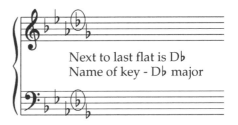

Next to last flat is Db
Name of key - Db major

Naming Flat Key Signatures Short-Cut

Music Application: Worksheet 28

Today's worksheet includes I AM THINE. This hymn tune is commonly used with "I Am Thine, O Lord."

Ear Training: See page 78.

In Rehearsal

1. Identify flat key signatures used in your music.

2. Review flat order.

CONCEPT CORNER

The previous session introduced key signatures. The tonal relationship of notes contains either all sharps or all flats. The exception is C major, which has no sharps or flats. The sharps or flats of the key signature alter all notes by the same name. For example, a key signature of one flat (Bb) indicates that all B's are flat throughout the piece.

Flats used in a key signature appear in a predetermined order. *Flat order* requires flats to be used as: Bb Eb Ab Db Gb Cb Fb. Therefore, if a key has three flats, it must be Bb, Eb, and Ab. Notice that flat order is the opposite (backward) of sharp order:

Sharps: F# C# G# D# A# E# B#
Flats: Bb Eb Ab Db Gb Cb Fb

Flat key signatures may be identified via the next-to-last flat in the key. Identify this flat to discover the name of the key. For example, a key signature with five flats (Bb Eb Ab Db Gb) has Db as the next-to-last flat. Therefore, the key is Db major. This short-cut always works. You have to memorize the key of F major since it has only one flat in the key signature (Bb).

Worksheet 28

Flat Key Signatures

1. Copy the flat order three times.

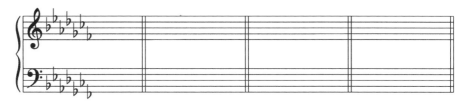

2. Name the following key signatures.
   (Hint: The next to last flat is the key.)

___   ___   ___   ___

3. Create the following key signatures.

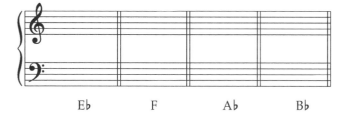

Eb   F   Ab   Bb

4. I AM THINE

   A. Circle the key signature.

   B. Name the key. _____

   C. Circle all Bb, Eb, Ab, and Db in the music.

   D. Clap and count the rhythm.

   E. Sing on scale numbers.

   F. Sing on text.

   *Bonus: How many measures are in this hymn? (Hint: the first full measure begins on "thine") _____

   *Bonus: What is the musical term for the partial measure at the beginning? _____

Preparation

1. Duplicate Closed and Open Score Examples (page 81).

2. Duplicate Worksheet 29.

Teaching Method

1. Distribute Closed and Open Score Examples to use with the following discussion.
   - Refrain from "Angels We Have Heard on High" (GLORIA).
   - Example demonstrates closed and open score.

2. Score
   - Term used for the printed page of music showing all of the ensemble parts.
   - Choral score shows the vocal parts and accompaniment.
   - Orchestral score shows the strings, winds, brass, and percussion parts.

3. Closed Score
   - Looks like a traditional hymn page or piano music.
   - Usually written on two staves:
     - √ One for female voices: soprano, alto
     - √ One for male voices: tenor, bass
   - Watch stem direction when parts divide.
     - √ Soprano and tenor = stems up
     - √ Alto and bass = stems down

4. Open Score
   - Each part has its own line.
   - Text may be written along with each part or shared between the lines.
   - Division of a part may appear as two notes stacked on top of each other; for example, soprano I and soprano II.

5. Reading the Score
   - Look for your part labeled at the beginning of the song.
   - Look through the song to locate your lines of music.
   - Notice special directions, such as "altos only" or "men."
   - Mark your music, as needed, to indicate your part.
   - Look for musical road map directions, such as D.C., D.S., repeats, and endings.

Music Application: Worksheet 29

Today's worksheet includes excerpts from two hymn tunes: JESU, JOY OF MAN'S DESIRING is commonly used with the title text; IRBY is commonly used with "Once in Royal David's City."

Ear Training: See page 78.

In Rehearsal

Discover how your choral scores are organized.
- Are they open or closed?
- Locate each part in the score.
- Identify special directions, such as "women only" or "solo."
- Mark your part, as needed.

CONCEPT CORNER

Choral score reading is critical to the success of your ensemble. It is important to be able to read and follow your part as well as the other parts around you. Knowing how the music fits together makes singing much easier and fun!

The *score* is the full printed page of music. Choral music typically shows all vocal parts as well as the accompaniment. This is helpful in finding your starting notes, counting measures of rest, and hearing how your part fits into the whole. Scores are standardized, usually moving from highest to lowest. Exceptions do exist, so always look for the part identification at the beginning of the music.

Closed score music resembles piano music or a traditional hymn page. Two staves contain both women's and men's parts. The soprano/alto parts are written on the top line; the tenor/bass parts on the lower line. Composers identify specific parts that contain unique rhythms by changing stem directions: soprano/tenor use stem up; alto/bass use stem down.

Open score assigns a specific line to each part. Divisions within a section occur when two or more notes are stacked on a single line. These indicate part I and part II, such as soprano I/soprano II.

Worksheet 29

Score Reading

1. Write the following music into open score.
   Place the soprano part on line 1, alto line 2, tenor line 3, and bass line 4.

2. Write the following music into closed score.
   Place the soprano and alto parts on line 1, tenor and bass on line 2.
   Watch stem direction when different rhythms occur on the same line.
   (Hint: Soprano and tenor stems up, alto and bass stems down.)

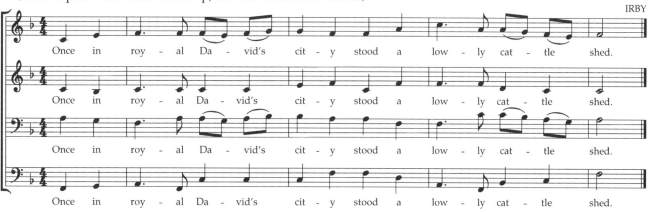

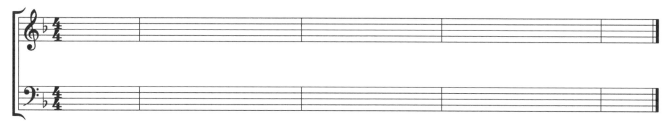

Preparation
1. Duplicate the Hymn Page Example *(inside front cover)*.

2. Duplicate Worksheet 30.

Teaching Method
1. Distribute the Hymn Page Example.
   - Hymn sample page: "Come, Thou Fount of Every Blessing (NETTLETON).
   - Example demonstrates a typical hymn page.

2. Discover information contained on a hymn page.

Title: "Come, Thou Fount of Every Blessing"
   - First line of text or poem title.
   - Does not refer to the melody.
   - Index: First Lines and Common Titles

Topic/Category: Personal Holiness
   - Subject area
   - Division or grouping in the hymnal
   - Index: Topics and Categories

Number: 400
   - Hymn number
   - May be different from page number.

Poet/Author: Robert Robinson
   - Poem written in 1758.
   - Index: Index of Composers, Arrangers, Authors, Translators, and Sources

Composer: Anonymous
   - Published in John Wyeth's *Repository of Sacred Music,* Part Second, 1813.
   - Index: Index of Composers, Arrangers, Authors, Translators, and Sources

Scripture Reference
   - Text based on 1 Samuel 7:12.
   - Index: Index of Scripture: Hymns, Canticles, Prayers, and Poems

Tune Name: NETTLETON
   - Appears in small upper case letters.
   - Name for the music/tune
   - Does not refer to the hymn text.
   - Index: Index of Tune Names

Meter: 87.87 D
   - Number of syllables per line/phrase doubled (D)

Come, thou Fount of every blessing (8)
tune my heart to sing thy grace; (7)
streams of mercy, never ceasing, (8)
call for songs of loudest praise (7)
Teach me some melodious sonnet, (8)
sung by flaming tongues above. (7)
Praise the mount! I'm fixed upon it, (8)
mount of thy redeeming love. (7)

   - Tunes with identical meters may be interchanged. You can sing this text with:
     BEECHER (Worksheet 12)
     EBENEZER (Worksheet 20)
     HYMN TO JOY (Worksheet 25)
     BRADBURY (Worksheet 27)
   - Index: Metrical Index

Music Application: Worksheet 30
   Today's worksheet includes LAUDA ANIMA. This hymn tune is commonly used with "Praise, My Soul, the King of Heaven," and "God, Whose Love Is Reigning O'er Us."

Ear Training: See page 78.

In Rehearsal
1. Practice the hymns for worship.

2. Identify parts of the hymn page.

3. Explore the indexes in your hymnal.

4. Learn more about the hymn; many books and online resources can provide this information.
   - Composer biography
   - Poet/author biography
   - Background on the hymn text

CONCEPT CORNER

The *hymn page* is full of helpful information regarding the song and text. Learning to decode the page helps you know more about the hymn. Each nugget is cross-referenced in multiple indexes, which allows you to find related material. The hymnal indexes are essential in locating a favorite hymn, finding scripture references, comparing meters and tunes, and planning worship. Your hymnal may contain other resources as well. Look through the pages to discover what riches are housed in your hymn book.

Worksheet 30
Hymn Page

Answer the following questions regarding this hymn.

1. Hymn title: _____

2. Composer: _____

3. Year the hymn tune was composed: _____

4. Poet/Author: _____

5. Year the poem was written: _____

6. Poem based on what scripture: _____

7. Hymn number: _____

8. Topic/Category: _____

9. Tune name: _____

10. Tune meter: _____

11. Write the first stanza on the hymn text as a poem, breaking each line at the metrical phrase.

    (Hint: The first line has eight syllables. You may use the back of this sheet.)

*Bonus: Locate the key signature and name the key: _____

*Bonus: What is the time signature:

THE GLORY OF THE TRIUNE GOD

66 — Praise, My Soul, the King of Heaven

WORDS: Henry F. Lyte, 1834 (Ps. 103)
MUSIC: John Goss, 1869

LAUDA ANIMA
87.87.87

EAR TRAINING

SESSION ONE

1. Identify the rhythm you hear in each example (use a metronome to establish a quarter pulse).
   - Leader plays 8 quarter notes; participants identify.
   - Leader plays 2 whole notes; participants identify.
   - Leader plays 4 half notes; participants identify.

2. Clap the rhythm you hear in each example.
   - Leader plays the following patterns in any order; participants clap the pattern in response.
3. Write the rhythm you hear in each example.
   - Leader plays the patterns in any order.
   - Participants write the rhythmic notation.

Session 1 — Ear Training: Note Values

SESSION TWO

1. Identify the rest you hear in each example (2.1). Use a metronome to establish a quarter pulse.

2. Clap the rhythm you hear in each example (2.2).
   - Leader plays the patterns in any order.
   - Participants clap the pattern in response.

3. Write the rhythm you hear in each example (2.2).
   - Leader plays the patterns in any order.
   - Participants write the rhythmic notation.

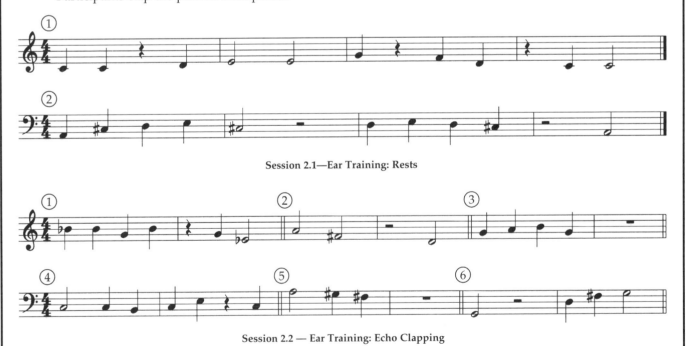

Session 2.1—Ear Training: Rests

Session 2.2 — Ear Training: Echo Clapping

Session Three

1. Clap the rhythm you hear in each example.
   - Leader plays the following patterns in any order.
   - Participants clap the pattern in response.

2. Write the rhythm you hear in each example.
   - Leader plays the patterns in any order.
   - Participants write the rhythmic notation.

Session 3 — Ear Training: Rhythm Examples

Session Four

1. 4/4 meter uses a strong-weak-strong-weak beat combination.

2. Walk the quarter pulse counting 1-2-3-4; be intentional in making beats 1 and 3 stronger.

3. Illustrate a 4/4 conducting pattern.

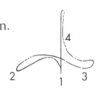

Session Five

Play the following examples in any order.
   - Participants **echo sing** the example.
   - Identify pitch movement: up, down, repeat.

Session 5 — Ear Training Playing Examples (Pitch Movement)

Session Six

Refer to the printed exercise on Worksheet 6.
   - Listen to each example. The leader plays the given pitch and one additional pitch. The second pitch will be one note higher or lower, or repeat.
   - Echo sing both notes.
   - Write the second pitch that is played.
   - Write the name of both pitches in the blanks.

Session 6 — Ear Training Playing Examples

SESSION SEVEN

Refer to the printed exercise on Worksheet 7.
- Listen to each example. The leader plays the given pitch and one additional pitch. The second pitch will be one note higher or lower, or repeat.
- Echo sing both notes.
- Write the second pitch that is played.
- Write the name of both pitches in the blanks.

Session 7 — Ear Training Playing Examples

SESSION EIGHT

Refer to the printed exercise on Worksheet 8.
- Listen to each example. The leader plays the given pitch and one additional pitch. The second pitch will be up or down a step, skip, or repeat.
- Echo sing both notes.
- Write the second pitch that is played.
- Write the name of both pitches in the blanks.

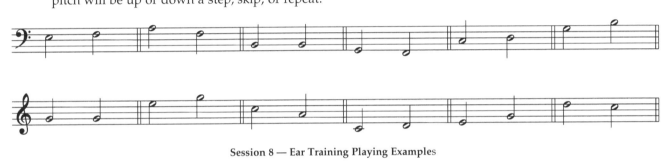

Session 8 — Ear Training Playing Examples

SESSION NINE

1. 3/4 meter uses a strong-weak-weak beat combination

2. Contrast 3/4 with 4/4, which uses a strong-weak-strong-weak beat combination.

3. Walk the quarter pulse, counting 1-2-3; be intentional in making beat 1 stronger.

4. Illustrate a 3/4 conducting pattern

5. Play any hymn in 3/4 as the participants conduct.

6. Listening exercise:
   - Leader plays the following examples in any order (page 71).
   - Participants identify the time signature of each example.

1. WINCHESTER OLD - From Est's *Psalter*, 1592

2. ST. AGNUS - John B. Dukes

3. BEALOTH - From Mason's *Sacred Harp*, 1843

4. ST. CHRYSOSTOM - Joseph Barnby

Session 9 — Ear Training Playing Examples

71

SESSION TEN

1. Play/sing various examples of melodic and harmonic 2nd and 3rd.

2. Play, then sing the following examples.

3. Ask: "Are the intervals 2nd, 3rd, or a combination of both?"

Session 10 — Ear Training Playing Examples

SESSION ELEVEN

1. Play/sing examples of melodic and harmonic 4th and 5th.

2. Play, then sing the following examples.

3. Ask: "Are the intervals 4th, 5th, or a combination of both?"

Session 11 — Ear Training Playing Examples

SESSION TWELVE

1. Play/sing examples of melodic and harmonic 6th, 7th, and octave.

2. Play, then sing the following examples.

3. Ask: "Are the intervals 6th, 7th, octave, or a combination?"

Session 12 — Ear Training Playing Examples

SESSION THIRTEEN

1. Play/sing examples of a natural note moving to a sharp.

2. Play/sing examples of a sharp note moving to a natural.

3. Listening exercise: bottom of Worksheet 13.
   - Leader plays the given pitch, then a second note.
   - Echo sing what the leader plays.
   - Write the appropriate accidental in front of the second note.
   - Write the names of both notes in the blanks.

Session 13 — Ear Training Playing Examples

72

SESSION FOURTEEN

1. Play/sing examples of a natural moving to a flat.

2. Play/sing examples of a flat moving to a natural.

3. Play/sing examples of a natural to a sharp.

4. Listening exercise: bottom of Worksheet 14
   - Leader plays the given pitch and a second note.
   - Echo sing what the leader plays.
   - Write the appropriate accidental in front of the second note (flat, natural, sharp).
   - Write the names of both notes in the blanks.

B   B♭   G♭   G♮   E   E♭   C   C♯   A♭   A♮   E   E♯   D♭   D♮   F   F♭

Session 14 — Ear Training Playing Examples

SESSION FIFTEEN

1. Review half steps: play/sing several examples.

2. Play/sing examples of notes moving up or down by half step.

3. Listening exercise: bottom of Worksheet 15.
   - Leader plays the given pitch and a second note.
   - Echo sing what the leader plays.
   - Write the second note.
   - Write the names of both notes in the blanks.

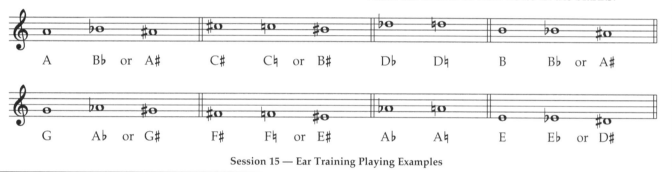

A   B♭ or A♯   C♯   C♮ or B♯   D♭   D♮   B   B♭ or A♯

G   A♭ or G♯   F♯   F♮ or E♯   A♭   A♮   E   E♭ or D♯

Session 15 — Ear Training Playing Examples

SESSION SIXTEEN

Listening example: bottom of Worksheet 16.
   - Leader establishes the quarter pulse and plays each example.

   - Participant writes in tie(s).
   - Clap and count each example.
   - Sing each example.

Session 16 — Ear Training Playing Examples

SESSION SEVENTEEN

1. 6/8 meter uses a strong-weak-weak–strong-weak-weak beat combination.
   - Walk the eighth note pulse: 1 2 3 4 5 6.
   - Be intentional in making beats 1 and 4 stronger.
   - Walk the dotted quarter pulse: 1 & a 2 & a (count in TWO).

2. Illustrate a 6/8 conducting pattern.

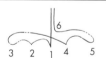

3. Play a hymn in 6/8 as the participants conduct.

4. Listening exercise: bottom of Worksheet 18.
   - Leader plays the following examples.
   - Participants identify time signature: 6/8 or 4/4.

continued on page 74

Session 17—Ear Training/Listening Playing Examples

SESSION EIGHTEEN

1. A blank staff line is included in Worksheet 18.

2. Leader claps measure 1.
   • Participants echo clap the pattern.
   • Participants write the rhythm pattern on their own paper.

3. Leader claps measure 2 and repeats the above process. Continue until all measures are demonstrated.

4. Participants clap all six measures of the exercise.

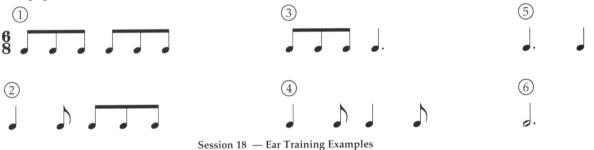

Session 18 — Ear Training Examples

SESSION NINETEEN

1. 2/2 meter uses a strong-weak beat combination.
   • Contrast 2/2 with 4/4.
   • Contrast 2/2 with 6/8.

2. Illustrate a 2/2 conducting pattern.

3. Play a hymn in 2/2 as the participants conduct.

4. Listening exercise
   • Leader plays the examples in any order.
   • Participants identify the time signature of each example: 2/2, 3/4, or 6/8.
   • Conduct each example.

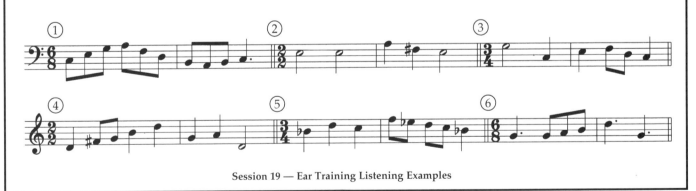

Session 19 — Ear Training Listening Examples

SESSION TWENTY

1. Echo clap each measure.
   - Listen for rhythmic accuracy.
   - Repeat, as needed.
   - Identify the time signature and type of triplet.

2. Count one measure to establish the pulse.
   - Leader claps each measure.
   - Participants write the rhythm.
   - Repeat each example as needed.

Session 20 — Ear Training Clapping Examples

SESSION TWENTY-ONE

1. Leader plays the examples in any order.

2. Participants identify the dynamic used in the example: *forte, piano,* or crescendo–diminuendo.

Session 21 — Ear Training Playing Examples

SESSION TWENTY-TWO

1. Review *staccato, fermata, tenuto,* and *accent*.
   - Demonstrate each articulation.

2. Listening Exercise: bottom of Worksheet 22.

3. Play the following examples in order.
   - Participants identify the articulation used and write it on the appropriate note(s).
   - Sing each example with the articulation.

Session 22 — Ear Training Playing Examples

SESSION TWENTY-THREE

1. Illustrate the repeat concept by echo singing the "Frere Jacques" melody on a nonsense syllable such as "pa" or on text.
   - Leader plays or sings the first measure.
   - Participants echo sing that measure (appears in the music as the second measure, indicated as cued notes).
   - Continue singing, alternating by measures.

2. Listening examples: Worksheet 23
   - Listen for the location of a repeat sign (Ex. 23.2).
   - Leader plays example, repeat as needed.
   - Participants write in the repeat sign.
   - Listen for the first and second endings (Ex. 23.3).
   - Leader plays example, repeat as needed.
   - Participants write in first and second endings.

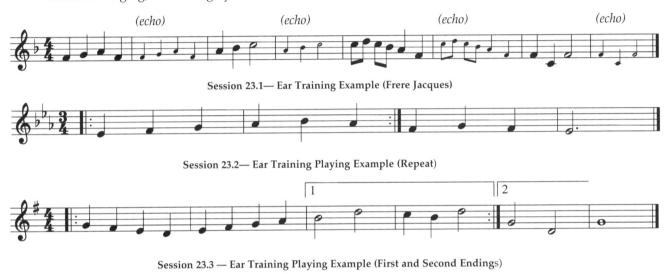

Session 23.1— Ear Training Example (Frere Jacques)

Session 23.2— Ear Training Playing Example (Repeat)

Session 23.3 — Ear Training Playing Example (First and Second Endings)

SESSION TWENTY-FOUR

1. Write the example on the board (Session 24.1).
   - Clap and count the rhythm.
   - Review definition of D.C. and D.S.

2. Leader claps Session 24.2 Rhythm Examples.
   - Participants determine if they hear *D.C. al fine* or *D.S. al fine.*

   - Participants insert music road map symbols.
   - All clap and count each example.

3. Participants create and add a two-measure coda.
   - Write in a *D.C. al coda.*
   - All clap and count the example again.

Session 24.1 — Ear Training Rhythm Example

Session 24.2 — Ear Training: Leader's Rhythm Examples

SESSION TWENTY-FIVE

1. Use HYMN TO JOY (Worksheet 25) for this exercise.
   - Leader plays the hymn, demonstrating a tempo mark of choice; participants identify the tempo.
   - Repeat, demonstrating a tempo change.

2. Leader plays each participant's version of the tune (Worksheet 25); participants identify tempo mark and changes used.

SESSION TWENTY-SIX

1. Play and sing the C major scale.

2. Review the pattern: (key note) W W H W W W H.

3. Leader plays the scale examples in any order.

- Participant identifies if each example is / is not a major scale.
- Indicate where the mistake occurs (if any); for example, "what sounds wrong."
- Sing the correct major scale.

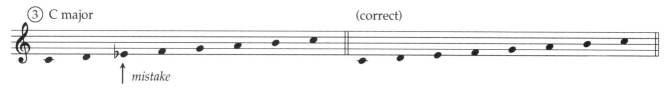

Session 26 — Ear Training Playing Examples

SESSION TWENTY-SEVEN

1. Sing major scales on numbers.

2. Sing intervals in a major scale.

3. Variation on singing intervals (previous example):

- Leader plays scale degree 1 (C).
- Participants sing alternating scale degree 2.
- Leader plays scale degree 1 (C).
- Participants sing alternating scale degree 3 (then 4, 5, and so forth).

Session 27— Ear Training Vocal Exercise

SESSION TWENTY-EIGHT

1. Sing major scales on numbers (1, 2, 3, 4, 5, 6, 7, 1, 7, 6, 5, 4, 3, 2, 1).

2. Sing intervals in a major scale.
   • Sing the pattern in different keys.
   • Sing *a cappella*.

3. Bonus: Add dynamics, such as *crescendo* (ascending) and *diminuendo* (descending).

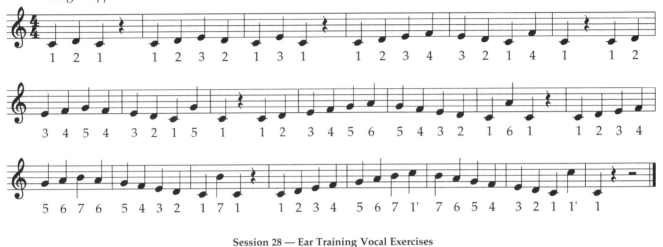

Session 28 — Ear Training Vocal Exercises

SESSION TWENTY-NINE

Learn to read and sing the hymn tunes on Worksheet 29.
   • Clap and count each part individually.
   • Assign participants a part.
   • Clap and count all four parts together.

• Sing each part individually, singing in your natural register (a comfortable octave).
• Sing as written with four-part harmony.

SESSION THIRTY

Discover hymn meter.
   • Leader reads a hymn text slowly by phrases; for example, use a hymn text from earlier worksheets.

• Participants count the number of syllables per line/phrase.
• When reading is completed, define the meter of the hymn text.

REPRODUCIBLE MUSIC EXAMPLES

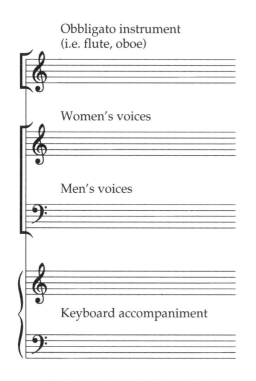

Obbligato instrument
(i.e. flute, oboe)

Women's voices

Men's voices

Keyboard accompaniment

Session 8 — Expanded Grand Staff

legato

staccato

fermata

tenuto

accent

Session 22 — Articulation Chart

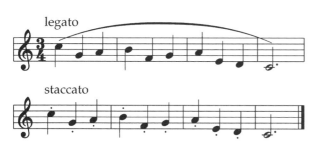

legato

staccato

Ex. 22.1 — Staccato Demonstration Example

tenuto

Ex. 22.3 — Tenuto Demonstration Example

fermata

Ex. 22.2 — Fermata Demonstration Example

accent

Ex. 22.4 — Accent Demonstration Example

Music Road Map Guide

Lead Me, Lord

1. D.C. al fine

Lead me, Lord, lead me in thy righ - teous-ness; make thy way

plain be - fore my face. For it is thou Lord thou, Lord

on - ly that mak - est me dwell in safe - ty.

2. D.S. al fine

Lead me, Lord, lead me in thy righ - teous-ness; make thy way

plain be - fore my face. For it is thou Lord thou, Lord

on - ly that mak - est me dwell in safe - ty.

mak - est me dwell in safe - ty.

WORDS: Psalm 5:8; 4:8
MUSIC: Samuel Sebastian Wesley

Session 24—Music Road Map

Closed Score

Open Score

Session 29 — Closed and Open Score Examples

ANSWER KEYS

Worksheet 1
Quarter, Half, and Whole Notes

1. Draw four examples of each note. Watch your stem direction.

2. HAMBURG

    A. Write the beats under each note.
    B. Clap and count the rhythm. (Do you see any patterns? Which lines use the same rhythm?) **Lines 1, 2, & 3**
    C. Count sing the rhythm.
    D. Sing the melody while tapping the quarter note pulse.
    E. What hymn text do you sing with this melody? **When I Survey the Wondrous Cross**

Worksheet 2
Quarter, Half, and Whole Rests

1. Draw four examples of each rest.

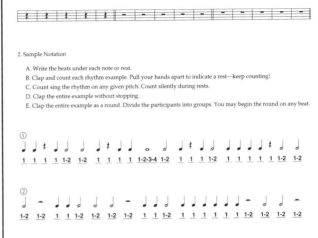

2. Sample Notation

    A. Write the beats under each note or rest.
    B. Clap and count each rhythm example. Pull your hands apart to indicate a rest—keep counting!
    C. Count sing the rhythm on any given pitch. Count silently during rests.
    D. Clap the entire example without stopping.
    E. Clap the entire example as a round. Divide the participants into groups. You may begin the round on any beat.

Worksheet 3
Eighth Notes/Rests and Sixteenth Notes/Rests

1. Draw four examples of each.

2. Rhythm Exercise

    A. Write the beats under each note. The first line is completed for you.
        For ♪ 𝄾 use 1 &. For ♫ use & a. (This will suffice for today's exercise.)
    B. Clap and count the rhythm.
    C. Count sing the rhythm.
    D. Sing the melody while tapping the quarter note pulse.
    E. Do you recognize this famous melody? **Hallelujah Chorus**

Worksheet 4
Time Signature

EASTER HYMN

    A. Write the 𝄴 time signature at the beginning of the first line.
    B. Draw in bar lines as indicated by the time signature.
    C. Draw a double bar line at the end of the hymn.
    D. Write the beats in the blanks below the music.
    E. Clap and count the rhythm.
    F. Count sing the hymn.
    G. What hymn text do you sing with this tune? **Jesus Christ is Risen Today**

Worksheet 5

Musical Staff

1. Number each line and space on the staff. Remember to number from bottom to top.

2. Identify the location of each note on the staff. L = line note, S = space note   Example: L4 S1

S1 L1 S2 L4 S3 L3 S2 L5 S4 L1 L2 L3 L4 L5 S1 S2 S3 S4

3. HERZLIEBSTER JESU

   A. Fill in the missing notes to complete the hymn.
   B. Identify note movement: up, down, repeat.
   C. Sing through the hymn.
   D. What hymn text do you sing with this tune?   **Ah, Holy Jesus**

2 quarter notes space 1   2 quarter notes space 2

quarter note line 3   2 quarter notes space 3

half note line 1   2 quarter notes line 1

half note line 2   half note space 1

Worksheet 6

Treble/G Clef

1. Fill in the missing letters moving left to right.

  ___   B   C   ___   E   ___

2. Fill in the missing letters moving right to left.

  ___   B   ___   D   ___   ___   G

3. Draw four treble/G clefs. Trace over the G line (line 2) with a dark pencil.

4. Write the note name below each pitch.

5. MORECAMBE

   A. Write the note name below each pitch.
   B. Identify if the notes move up, down, or repeat.
   C. How many measures are in this hymn? ____
   D. Sing the note names with this hymn tune.
   E. What hymn text do you sing with this tune? _____

6. Ear Training

   A. Write the second pitch that is played.
   B. Write the name of both pitches in the blanks.

Worksheet 7

Bass/F Clef

1. Draw four bass/F clefs. Trace over the F line (line 4) with a dark pencil.

2. Write the note name below each pitch.

C   A   G   G   F   D   A   C   B   E

3. STUTTGART

   A. Write the note name below each pitch.
   B. Identify if the notes move up, down, or repeat.
   C. How many measures are in this hymn?   **8**
   D. Sing the note names with this hymn tune.
   E. What hymn text do you sing with this tune?   **Child of Blessing, Child of Promise**
      Come, Thou Long Expected Jesus
      O My Soul, Bless God the Father

G   G   C   C   D   D   E   C   G   G   A   F   D   G   E

E   E   D   E   C   D   C   B   C   A   G   C   C   B   C

4. Ear Training

   A. Write the second pitch that is played.
   B. Write the name of both pitches in the blanks.

C   C   F   E   G   A   D   E

G   A   B   B   E   D   A   G

Worksheet 8

Grand Staff

1. Complete 4 examples of the grand staff. Include brace, bar line, treble clef, and bass clef.

2. Draw the missing half note. Write the names of both notes in the blanks.

skip ↑   step ↓   skip ↓   step ↑   repeat   skip ↑   step ↓

A   C   E   D   B   G   E   F   C   C   D   F   D   C

step ↑   skip ↑   repeat   step ↓   repeat   skip ↓   step ↑

B   C   A   C   G   G   D   C   F   F   A   F   A   B

3. ADORO TE DEVOTE

   A. Circle your response above each example: step, skip, repeat.
   B. Sing the note names with this tune.
   C. What hymn text do you sing with this tune?   **Humbly I Adore Thee**

4. Ear Training

E   F   A   F   B   B   G   F   C   D   G   B

G   G   E   G   C   A   C   D   E   G   D   C

83

Worksheet 9

3/4 Meter

1. Write the count/beats in the blanks below each note/rest.

2. Add one A to complete each measure.

3. MARYTON

    A. Write the 3/4 time signature at the beginning of the first line.
    B. Draw in bar lines as indicated by the time signature.
    C. Draw a double bar line at the end of the hymn.
    D. Write the beats in the blanks below the music.
    E. Clap and count the rhythm.
    F. Count sing the hymn.
    G. What hymn text do you sing with this tune? **O Master, Let Me Walk with Thee**

Worksheet 10

Intervals: 2nds and 3rds

1. Draw the missing melodic interval pitch as indicated by the arrow.
2. Write the note names in the blanks.

3. Draw the missing harmonic interval pitch below the given note.
4. Write the note names in the boxes.

5. TRENTHAM

    A. Circle and label the following intervals: harmonic 2nd (H2) and harmonic 3rd (H3)
    B. Clap and count this hymn tune.
    C. Sing this hymn tune.
    D. What hymn text do you sing with this tune? **Breathe on Me, Breath of God**

Worksheet 11

Intervals: 4ths and 5ths

1. Draw the missing melodic interval pitch as indicated by the arrow.
2. Write the note names in the blanks.

3. Draw the missing harmonic interval pitch above the given note.
4. Write the note names in the boxes.

5. HURSLEY

    A. Circle and label the following intervals: harmonic 2nd (H2), 3rd (H3), 4th (H4), and 5th (H5)
    B. Clap and count this hymn tune; review 3/4 meter.
    C. Sing this hymn tune.
    D. What hymn text do you sing with this tune? **Come, Sinners, to the Gospel Feast**

Worksheet 12

Intervals: 6ths, 7ths, and 8va (octave)

1. Draw the missing melodic interval pitch as indicated by the arrow.
2. Write the note names in the blanks.

3. Draw the missing harmonic interval pitch below the given note.
4. Write the note names in the boxes.

5. BEECHER

    A. Circle and label examples of harmonic 6th (H6), 7th (H7), and octave (H8).
    B. Clap and count this hymn tune.
    C. Sing this hymn tune.
    D. What hymn text do you sing with this tune? **Love Divine, All Loves Excelling**

84

Worksheet 13
Sharp and Natural

1. Draw four sharps on different lines. Draw four sharps on different spaces.

2. Draw four naturals on different lines. Draw four naturals on different spaces.

3. Add a sharp in front of each note.
4. Write the note name in the blank.

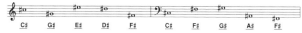

C# G# E# D# F# C# F# G# A# F#

5. REST

   A. Draw a circle around each sharp.
   B. Draw a box around each natural.
   C. Write the name of each note in the blank.
   D. Sing the hymn tune.
   E. What hymn text do you sing with this tune? **Dear Lord and Father of Mankind**

E E E D# E G G F# F♮ E C C D D E E F G C

C B A A A G F F# G F E G C C C D E

6. Ear Training
The leader will play the first note followed by the second note.
   A. Add the appropriate accidental (♯ or ♮) to the second note.
   B. Write the names of both notes in the blanks.

A A# C# C♮ F F# E# E♮ C C# D D# B# B♮ G G#

Worksheet 14
Flat

1. Draw four flats on different lines. Draw four flats on different spaces.

2. Add a flat in front of each note.
3. Write the note name in the blank.

B♭ E♭ A♭ A♭ G♭ E♭ E♭ C♭ G♭ B♭

4. DEO GRACIAS

   A. Draw a circle around each flat.
   B. Sing the hymn tune.
   C. What hymn text do you sing with this tune? **O Love, How Deep**

5. Ear Training
The leader will play the first note followed by the second note.
   A. Add the appropriate accidental (♭, ♯, ♮) to the second note.
   B. Write the names of both notes in the blanks.

B B♭ G♭ G♮ E E♭ C C# A A♭ E E# D♭ D♮ F F♭

Worksheet 15
Enharmonic

1. Draw the enharmonic equivalent for each example. Write the name of both notes in the blanks.

A# / B♭   F / E#   D♭ / C#   B / C♭   G# / A♭   E♭ / D#   F# / G♭   F♭ / E

2. This familiar hymn tune has been set with odd accidentals.
   A. Rewrite the hymn using the enharmonic spelling for each circled note.
   B. Sing the hymn looking at version 1.
   C. Sing the hymn looking at version 2.
   D. Which setting seems easier to read/sing? __2__ Why? **(Student's opinion, such as fewer accidentals, etc.)**
   E. What hymn text do you sing with this tune? **Jesus Loves Me**

Version 1:

Version 2:

3. Ear Training
The leader will play the given note and one other note 1/2 step up or down.
   A. Sing the example you hear played.
   B. Write the second note which is played.
   C. Write the names of both notes in the blanks. *(Note to leader: Student may write enharmonic).*

A / B♭   C# / C♮   D♭ / D♮   B / B♭   G / G#   F# / F♮   A♭ / A♮   E / E♭

Worksheet 16
Slur and Tie

1. Identify each example as a slur or a tie. Write your response in the blank.

slur   tie   slur   tie   tie   slur   slur   tie

2. Draw a slur over each measure. 3. Draw a slur under each measure.

4. Musical Math: Draw a tie in each example. Write the combined note value (♩) in the blank. ♩ o = __5__

♩ ♩ = __4__   ♩ ♩ = __3__   ♪ ♩ = __1 1/2__   o ♩ = __6__   ♩ ♩ = __2__   ♩. ♩ = __5__

5. Note to note: Draw a tie in each example. Write an equivalent note in the blank.   ♩ ♩ = ♩.

♩ ♩ = ♩   ♪ ♪ = ♩   ♩ ♩ = o   ♩ ♩ ♩ = ♩.   ♩ ♩ ♩ ♩ = o

6. MARTYRDOM

   A. Draw a circle around each slur.
   B. Draw a box around each tie.
   C. Clap and count the rhythm.
   D. Sing with the text. Notice how the slurs indicate a single syllable.

A - las! and did my Sav - ior bleed, and did my Sov - ereign die? _____ Would

he de - vote that sa - cred head for sin - ners such as I? _____

7. Ear Training: Listen for the tie(s) in each example. Write in the tie(s) you hear.

①   ②   ③   ④

Worksheet 17

⁶⁄₈ Meter

1. Write the beats in the blanks below each measure.

1　2　3　4-5-6　1-2　3　4　5　6　1-2　3　4-5　6　1　2　3　4　5 & 6

1　2-3　4　5-6　1-2　3　4　5-6　1　2　3 & 4-5　6　1-2-3-4-5-6

2. Add one C to complete each measure.

3. IN DULCI JUBILO

A. Write the ⁶⁄₈ time signature at the beginning of the first line.
B. Draw in bar lines as indicated by the time signature.
C. Draw a double bar line at the end of the hymn.
D. Write the beats in the blanks below the music.
E. Clap and count the rhythm.
F. Count sing the hymn.
G. What hymn text do you sing with this tune?　**Good Christian Friends, Rejoice**
*Bonus: Circle the slurs; draw a box around the tie.

1-2-3　4　5　6　1-2　3　4-5　6　1-2　3　4-5　6　1-2　3　4-5　6　1-2　3　4-5-6　1-2　3　4-5　6

1-2　3　4-5　6　1-2　3　4-5-6　1-2　3　4-5　6　1-2　3　4-5　6　1-2　3　4-5　6

1-2　3　4-5　6　1-2　3　4-5-6　1-2　3　4-5　6　1-2-3　4-5　6　1-2　3　4-5　6　1-2-3-4-5　6

Worksheet 18
Dotted Eighth/Sixteenth and Pickup

1. Draw four examples of ♪♫ in the measures.

2. Pick-up: Write the beats under each example. Watch the time signature.

① ② ③ ④ ⑤ ⑥

4　1 2 3-4　5-6　1 2 3 4-5-6　3　1 & 2 3　6　1 2 & 3 4 5 6　&　1 2 & 3　3-4　1 2-3 4 &

3. GREENSLEEVES

A. Draw a box around the pickup measure.
B. Circle each ♪♫
C. Write the rhythm/beats in the blanks.
D. How many beats are in the final measure?　**5**　Why?　beat 6 is at beginning (pickup)
E. Write the name of each sharped note.
F. Clap and count the rhythm.
G. Sing.

6　1-2　3　4-5 & 6　1-2　3　4-5 & 6　1-2　3　4-5 & 6　1-2　3　4-5　6
What child is this who laid to rest, on Ma-ry's lap is sleep-ing? Whom

1-2　3　4-5 & 6　1-2　3　4-5 & 6　1-2　3　4-5 & 6　1-2　3　4-5-6
an-gels greet with an-thems sweet while shep-herds watch are keep-ing?

1-2-3　4-5 & 6　1-2　3　4-5 & 6　1-2　3　4-5 & 6　1-2　3　4-5-6
This, this is Christ the King, whom shep-herds guard and an-gels sing;

1-2-3　4-5 & 6　1-2　3　4-5 & 6　1-2　3　4-5 & 6　1-2-3　4-5
haste, haste to bring him laud, the babe, the son of Ma - ry.

4. Ear Training: Each example is one measure in ⁶⁄₈.

Worksheet 19
²⁄₂ Meter; cut time

1. Write the beats in the blanks below each note/rest.

1 & 2 &　1　2　1 & a 2　1　2　1 e & 2 &　1-2　&　1　2　&　1-2

2. Choose the correct time signature for each example: ²⁄₂　³⁄₄　or ⁶⁄₈
   A. Write your answer (time signature) on each example.
   B. Write the beats in the blanks below each measure.

① ② ③

1　&　2　1　&　2　1-2-3　4-5-6　1　2　3　4-5-6　1　2　3　1　2　3

④ ⑤ ⑥

1　2　3　4　5　6　1　2　3　4-5-6　1-&　2　&　1　2　3　1　2　3

3. DUKE STREET

A. Draw in bar lines are indicated by the time signature.
B. Draw a double bar line at the end of the hymn.
C. Write the beats in the blanks below the music.
D. Clap and count the rhythm.
E. Count sing the hymn.
F. What hymn text do you sing with this tune?　From all that Dwell Below the Skies / Jesus Shall Reign / Forth in Thy Name, O Lord / I Know that My Redeemer Lives
*Bonus: Circle the slurs.

1　2　&　2　&　1　2　&　1-2　1　2　&
1　2　&　2　1-2　&　1　&　2　&
1　&　2　&　1-2　1　2　&　1-2　&　2　1-2

Worksheet 20
Triplet

1. Turn these quarter notes into eighth note triplets.

2. Turn these quarter notes into quarter note triplets.

3. EBENEZER

A. Draw in bar lines. Remember: the quarter triplets receive one beat in ⁴⁄₂ meter.
B. Draw a double bar line at the end of the hymn.
C. Write the beats in the blanks.
D. Clap and count the rhythm.
E. Count sing the hymn.
F. What hymn text do you sing with this tune?　God Hath Spoken by the Prophets / Let My People Seek Their Freedom / Once to Every Man and Nation
*Bonus: Which three lines of this hymn are identical?　**1, 2, 4**
How does this information help you as a musician?　reduces the amount of music to learn, hymn is only two lines

1　2-trip-let 3　1　2-trip-let 3　a　4　1　2-trip-let 3　a 4　1　a　2　3-4
1　2-trip-let 3　4　1　2-trip-let 3　a　4　1　2-trip-let 3　a 4　1　a　2　3-4
1　2-trip-let 3　4　1　2-trip-let 3　4　1　2-trip-let 3　4　1　2-trip-let 3-4
1　2-trip-let 3　4　1　2-trip-let 3　a　4　1　2-trip-let 3　a 4　1　a　2　3-4

Worksheet 21

Dynamics

1. Arrange these dynamic abbreviations from soft to loud: *mf* *p* *pp* *f* *mp* *ff*

pp *p* *mp* *mf* *f* *ff*

2. Match the Italian dynamic in Column A with the English in Column B.

Column A	Column B
piano	moderately soft
mezzo forte	loud
forte	very soft
mezzo piano	soft
pianissimo	very loud
fortissimo	moderately loud

3. STEAL AWAY

  A. Circle the dynamics.
  B. Write the beats in the blanks.
  C. Clap and count the rhythm. Repeat incorporating the dynamics.
  D. Count sing the rhythm incorporating the dynamics.
  E. Sing on text incorporating the dynamics.
  *Bonus: Circle the triplets.

Worksheet 22

Articulation

1. Draw the designated articulation above or below each note. (*Note: The fermata is usually above the staff.*)

staccato   fermata   tenuto   accent

2. Hymn excerpts demonstrate the four articulation signs in this lesson.
  A. Circle the articulation signs used in each example, such as the staccato marks in the first line.
  B. Speak each example using the articulation indicated.
  C. Sing each example using the articulation indicated.

Staccato — AMEN, AMEN
A - men, a - men, a - men, a - men, a - men!

Fermata — THOMPSON
Come home, come home; you who are wea-ry, come home!
earn - est-ly, ten - der - ly, Je - sus is call-ing, call-ing, O sin-ner, come home!

Tenuto — UNSER HERRSCHER
God of love and God of power, thou hast called us for this hour.

Accent — DARWALL'S 148th
Lift up your heart, lift up your voice; re - joice; a-gain I say, re - joice.

3. Ear Training: Add the appropriate articulation(s) to each example—staccato, fermata, tenuto, or accent.

①   ④
②   ⑤
③   ⑥

Worksheet 23

Repeats, First and Second Endings

1. Rewrite the following example using a repeat sign.
  Hint: Look for a measure containing music you have seen. Then, compare the music following to determine if a repeat sign may be used.

IN DIR IST FREUDE

In thee is glad - ness, a - mid all sad - ness, Je - sus, sun - shine of my heart.

By thee are giv - en the gifts of heav - en, thou the true Re - deem - er art.

2. First and second endings are used in the following example.
  Rewrite this hymn refrain in full, as you would sing it, without the endings.
  What is the total number of measures in this refrain? __8__

WORDS OF LIFE

Beau - ti - ful words, won - der - ful words, Won - der - ful words of Life. Life.

3. Ear Training
  A. Listen as the following example is played. Draw the missing repeat sign.

  B. Listen as the following example is played. Draw the missing first and second endings.

Worksheet 24

D.C. and D.S.

1. Draw a line from each term in Column A to the appropriate definition in Column B.

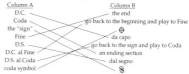

Column A	Column B
D.C.	go back to the beginning and play to Fine
Coda	⊕
the "sign"	da capo
Fine	go back to the sign and play to Coda
D.S.	an ending section
D.C. al Fine	dal segno
D.S. al Coda	𝄋
coda symbol	

2. ST. THEODULPH

  A. Circle the time signature.
  B. This hymn begins on what beat? __4__
  C. The first not of the refrain is called a(n) **pickup** (its musical function, not the note name) **(upbeat, anacrusis)**
  D. What is the last word sung in the hymn? **ring**
  E. What is the first word sung after the D.C.? **All**
  F. How many times is the refrain sung? **6 times**
  G. How many measures are in the refrain? __8__
    (*Hint: measure one begins on "glory"*)
  H. Name and define the symbol ♮ used in measures 9, 10, and 11. **natural - moves note up from E♭**
  I. Clap and count the rhythm.
  J. Count sing the melody (or parts).
  K. Sing the hymn on text.

All Glory, Laud, and Honor

Refrain
All glo - ry, laud, and hon - or, to thee, Re - deem - er, King, to whom the lips of chil - dren made

Fine
sweet ho - san - nas ring.

1. Thou art the King of Is - ra - el, thou Da - vid's roy - al
2. The com - pa - ny of an - gels are prais - ing thee on
3. The peo - ple of the He - brews with psalms be - fore thee
4. To thee, be - fore thy pas - sion, they sang their hymns of
5. Thou didst ac - cept their prais - es; ac - cept the prayers we

D.C.
Son, who in the Lord's name com - est, the King and Bless - ed One.
high, and we with all cre - a - tion in cho - rus make re - ply.
went; our prayer and praise and an - thems be - fore thee we pre - sent.
praise; to thee, now high ex - alt - ed, our mel - o - dy we raise.
bring, who in all good de - light - est, thou good and gra - cious King.

Worksheet 25
Tempo Marks

1. Arrange the following tempo marks from slowest to fastest.

Moderato	Adagio	Allegro	Vivace	Largo	Andante
Largo	**Adagio**	**Andante**	**Moderato**	**Allegro**	**Vivace**

2. Define each tempo mark. Write the correct definition number in the blank beside each term.

3 Allegro	1. moderately slow, walking tempo		
5 Moderato	2. very slow, broad		
1 Andante	3. fast		
2 Largo	4. slow		
6 Vivace	5. moderately		
4 Adagio	6. lively		

3. Define each tempo change. Write the correct definition number in the blank beside each term.

3 accelerando	1. freely, flexible tempo
1 rubato	2. gradually slower
4 a tempo	3. gradually faster
2 rallentando	4. return to normal speed

4. Be the composer. Add the following items to the hymn. Sing your version!
   A. Select a tempo mark and write it above the first measure.
   B. Select a tempo change and write it somewhere within the body of the hymn.
   C. Write "a tempo" shortly after the previous tempo change.
   D. Write "rall." (rallentando) near the end.
   *Bonus: Share your version with other participants.

choice of participant

HYMN TO JOY

Joy - ful, joy - ful, we a - dore thee, God of glo - ry, Lord of love; hearts un - fold like flowers be - fore thee

o - pening to the sun a - bove. Melt the clouds of sin and sad - ness, drive the dark of

doubt a - way. Giv - er of im - mor - tal glad - ness, fill us with the light of day!

Worksheet 26
Major Scale

1. The pattern for a major scale is (key note) W W H W W W H.
   A. Create a major scale starting on D.
   B. Label the key note and intervals (whole and half steps).
   C. Label the scale degrees (1, 2, 3, …).

1 2 3 4 5 6 7 1

W W H W W W H

2. Each scale has one mistake.
   A. Circle the mistake.
   B. Write the correct note in its place.

① ② ③ ④

3. ANTIOCH
   A. The melody of this hymn contains a complete descending scale. Locate and circle the scale.
   B. Two partial descending scales are also used in the melody. Locate and circle these.
   C. What is the letter name of this scale? **D**
   D. Clap and count the rhythm.
   E. The scale degrees are listed below each note. Sing this familiar hymn tune on scale numbers.
   F. What text do you sing with this tune? **Joy to the World**
   *Bonus: An octave leap is used in this melody. Find it and draw a box around it.

1 7 6 5 4 3 2 1 5 6 6 7 7 1

1 7 6 5 4 3 1 1 7 6 5 4 3 3 3 3 3 4

5 4 3 2 2 2 3 4 3 2 1 1 6 5 4 3 4 3 2 1

Worksheet 27
Sharp Key Signatures

1. Copy the sharp order three times.

2. Name the following key signatures.
   (Hint: The key is 1/2 step higher than the last sharp.)

G **A** **B** **D**

3. Create the following key signatures.

E G A D

4. BRADBURY
   A. Circle the key signature.
   B. Name the key. **D**
   C. Circle all F♯ and C♯ in the music.
   D. Clap and count the rhythm.
   E. Sing on scale numbers.
   F. Sing on text.
   *Bonus: Which two lines sound identical? **1, 2**
   *Bonus: What musical symbol is used three measures from the end? **fermata**

3 3 4 3 5 3 2 3 4 6 5 4 5

Sav - ior, like a shep - herd lead us, much we need thy ten - der care;

3 3 2 3 4 3 5 5
in thy pleas-ant pas-tures feed us, for our use thy folds pre - pare. Bless - ed

6 1 7 6 5 3 3 3 2 6 5 4 3 5 5
Je - sus, bless-ed Je - sus! Thou hast bought us, thine we are. Bless - ed

6 1 7 6 5 1 2 3 5 4 2 1
Je - sus, bless-ed Je - sus! Thou has bought us, thine we are.

Worksheet 28
Flat Key Signatures

1. Copy the flat order three times.

2. Name the following key signatures.
   (Hint: The next to last flat is the key.)

A♭ **B♭** **D♭** **E♭**

3. Create the following key signatures.

E♭ F A♭ B♭

4. I AM THINE
   A. Circle the key signature.
   B. Name the key. **A♭**
   C. Circle all B♭, E♭, A♭, and D♭ in the music.
   D. Clap and count the rhythm.
   E. Sing on scale numbers.
   F. Sing on text.
   *Bonus: How many measures are in this hymn? (Hint: the first full measure begins on "thine") **16**
   *Bonus: What is the musical term for the partial measure at the beginning? **pickup (upbeat, anacrusis)**

3 4 3 2 2 2 3 2 1 1 1 7 6 6 1 6 5 3 4
I am thine, O Lord, I have heard thy voice, and it told thy love to me; but I

5 3 2 1 7 6 5 1 7 6 1 4 3 2 3 4
long to rise in the arms of faith and be clos - er drawn to thee. Draw me

5 3 2 1 7 6 5 1 7 6 1 4 3 2 3 4
near - er, near - er, bless-ed Lord, to the cross where thou hast died. Draw me

5 5 3 3 2 1 7 6 5 1 7 6 1 4 3 2 1
near - er, near - er, near-er, bless-ed Lord, to thy pre - cious, bleed - ing side.